A SALMON FOR THE SCHOOLHOUSE

SOURCES IN LOCAL HISTORY No3

The *Sources in Local History* series is sponsored by the *European Ethnological Research Centre* c/o the National Museums of Scotland, Queen Street, Edinburgh EH2 1JD

General Editor: Alexander Fenton

'In later Times, I hope the people of Ardclach may enjoy reading a description of much that doubtless will be considered old-fashioned in their time.'

Mrs Elsie Thomson 20 March 1900

A SALMON FOR THE SCHOOLHOUSE

A Nairnshire Parish in the Nineteenth Century

From the diaries of Robert and Elsie Thomson

Edited by
John Love and Brenda McMullen

CANONGATE ACADEMIC
in association with
The European Ethnological Research Centre
and the National Museums of Scotland

Sources in Local History No 3

First published in 1994 by
Canongate Academic, an imprint of Canongate Press Ltd,
14 Frederick Street, Edinburgh EH2 2HB

British Library Cataloguing in Publication Data

A catalogue record for this book is available on request from the British Library

ISBN 1 89841 019 4

Typeset by Hewer Text Composition Services, Edinburgh
Printed and bound by Cromwell Press, Melksham Wiltshire

Contents

Plate Section

For the people of Ardclach and Glenferness, especially
Mr and Mrs F. Masson, and the late
Mr and Mrs J. Macbean, who were
such good friends and inspiration.

MAP 1

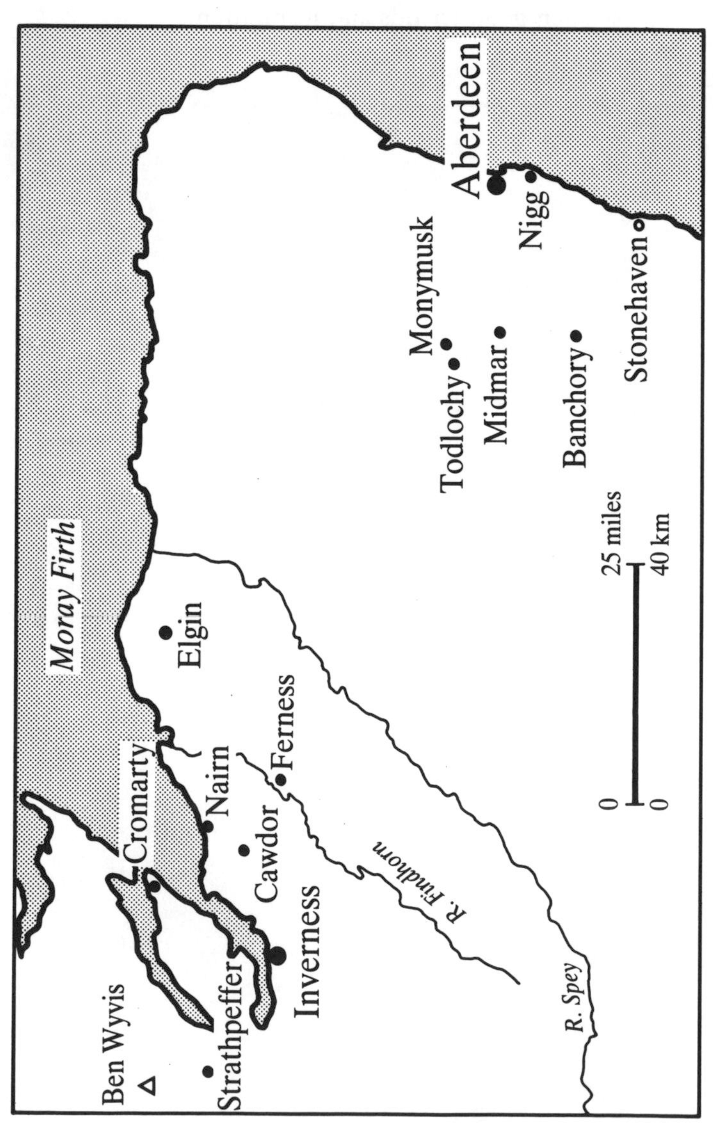

North-East Scotland

MAP 2

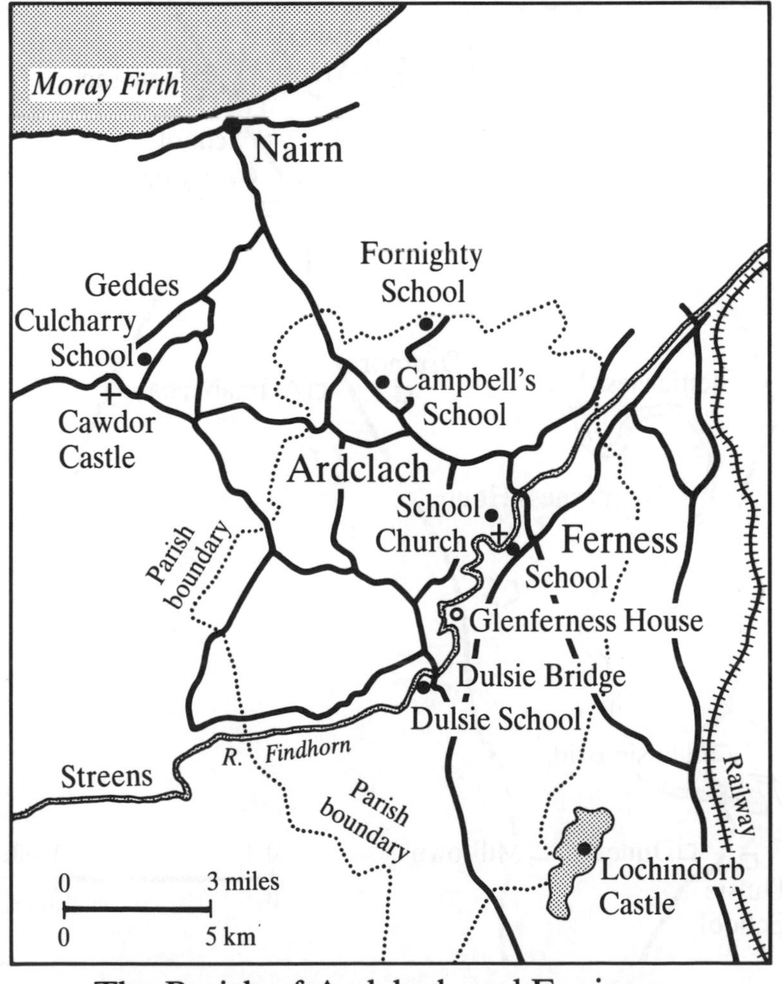

The Parish of Ardclach and Environs

MAP 3

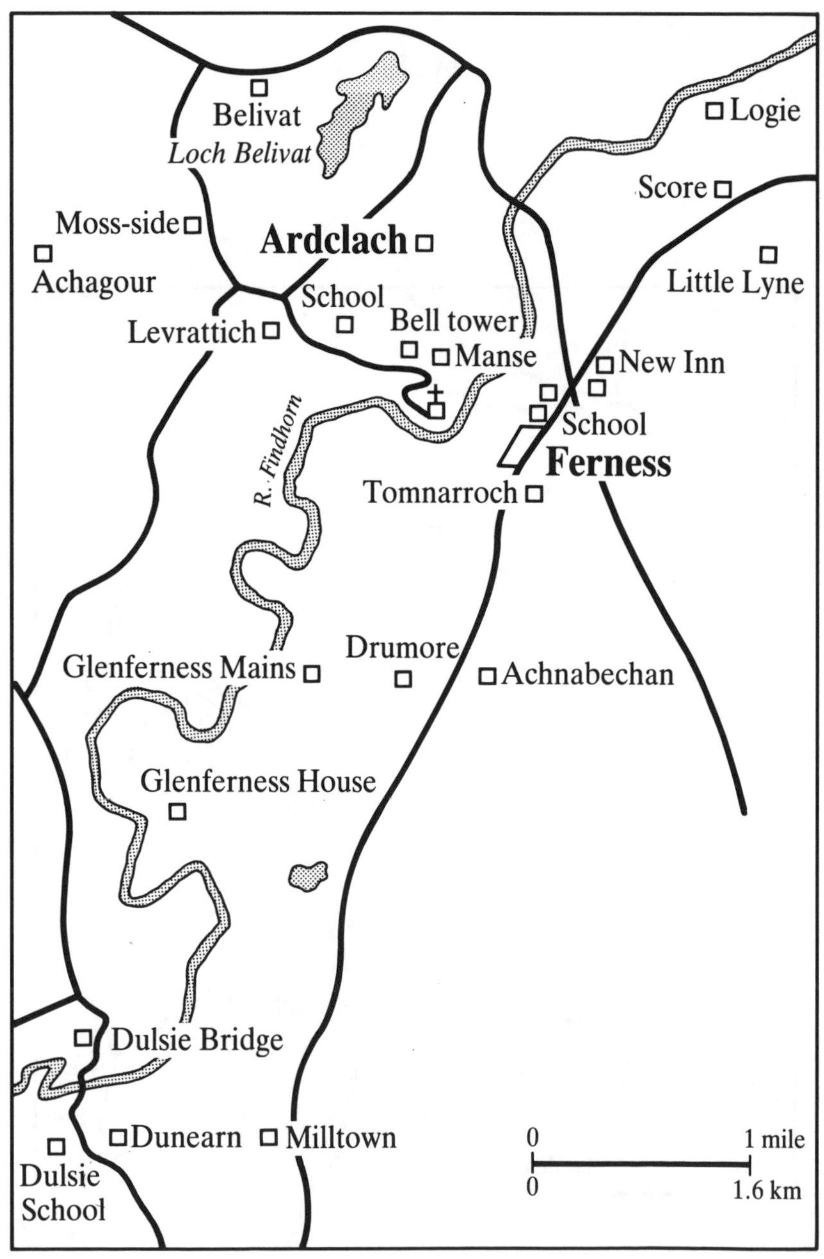

Ardclach and Ferness

Preface

I have been asked by John Love and Brenda McMullen, who have so cleverly compiled this book from my grandparents' Diaries, to write a preface. This I willingly do and dedicate the book with love to my dear father and grandfather who left this world too early for me to appreciate their worthiness.

Mrs Helen Lamb

Introduction

'At Nairn we may fix the verge of the Highlands; for here I first saw peat fires, and first heard the Gaelic language.' So wrote Dr Johnson as he travelled westwards across Scotland in 1773. Nowadays Gaelic survives only in the placenames of Nairnshire. Ardclach, its largest parish, means 'the height of the stones'. In 1891 there were still 205 people living in this part of rural Nairnshire who could speak Gaelic, and one old lady who knew only Gaelic, having no English at all. This census recorded about 950 parishioners altogether. The area consists mainly of hill farmland and heather moor and it is bisected by the river Findhorn.

The Findhorn is one of the most beautiful but relatively little-known rivers in Scotland. It parallels the more famous river Spey in a spectacular sixty-mile course, to empty into the Moray Firth only ten or so miles to the west of Speymouth. For half its length – from the Streens near Tomatin, to the Sluie a mere five miles from the sea – the Findhorn is hidden in a deep granite gorge, difficult of access and clothed in wild, almost primeval forest. In a shady hollow by the riverside stands the Ardclach parish church, dating from 1626 but too close to the noisy torrent, it was deemed, for its bell to be heard by the faithful. And so the belfry was built on a hill nearby. Its peal gave the local community warning of cattle raiders sallying forth from the Streens. The historic bell tower is now an ancient monument and the church has recently fallen into disuse. The congregation now use the former Free Church built in 1844 at Crask, only a mile and a half away. At this hub of Ardclach's upland farmsteads was also built the parish school, probably early in the eighteenth century. It was here that Robert and Elsie Thomson came to be appointed in 1874.

Robert Thomson was born in Aberdeenshire in 1838 – the sixth generation of his family to bear that name. His father had been widowed at an early date, none of his three children surviving. In his 71st year Robert Thomson senior remarried; his new wife, Mary Urquhart, was only half his age. They had two boys – Robert, the subject of this narrative, and Alexander, who never saw his first birthday. Robert senior died aged 76 and his widow ultimately came to live with her son in the schoolhouse at Cawdor where she died, aged 70, in September 1870.

As a schoolboy Robert junior had gained an interest in astronomy from his teacher. Although a telescope was hopelessly beyond the reach of both his own means and that of his parents, he and a friend David Moir set about grinding lenses to make such an instrument of their own. From his earliest boyhood he also confessed to 'a peculiar delight in the study of birds, insects and plants'.

In 1856, while training to be a teacher in Glasgow, Robert took up entomology seriously and during his first season had collected about a dozen species of butterflies. The following year he gained a temporary post on the coast of Kincardine, before taking an appointment as Free Church teacher at Culcharry School near Cawdor in Nairnshire. 'In a few years my cabinet contained specimens of seventeen different butterflies, and one hundred and sixty species of moths belonging to the district.'

But in addition to his entomological and botanical pursuits, Robert found time to woo a local girl, Elsie Fraser. They were wed on 4 September 1862, he at the age of 24 and his bride three years younger. Almost exactly a year later their first child was born, Elsie Mary Moir, and a son, Robert, followed on 30 December 1865.

The family moved to Ardclach Parish School at the commencement of 1874. This was one of several schools serving the parish, and it might be useful here to mention a little of their history.

Sometime in the eighteenth century the Scottish Society for the Propagation of Christian Knowledge (SSPCK) had established an institution at Fornighty, where Ardclach marches with the neighbouring parish of Auldearn. SSPCK schools had been set up in many rural districts where no other education was available. They were, however, as one historian has observed, more inclined 'towards instructing children in the principles of Christianity rather than towards elevating their intellectual and secular interests'. Society teachers were usually less qualified and less privileged than their parochial colleagues. They were not normally permitted to collect fees from their pupils but could accept only donations towards the Society. Their Saturday afternoons were to be spent in catechising the poor of the parish.

By 1792, when the Old Statistical Account of Scotland was compiled, the SSPCK school at Fornighty accommodated some 50 pupils from the north end of Ardclach parish. Nearby, Mrs Brodie of Lethen had also established a spinning school for young girls.

Ardclach Parish School is also mentioned in the Statistical Account but it is not known when it actually came into existence. By 1792 it had attracted 40 scholars from the southern inland reaches of the district. The schoolmaster at that time was Alexander Falconer, who received a salary of £10 per annum in addition to any scholars' fees which he might succeed in collecting, usually paid in kind – some chickens or a sack of meal. When he finally laid down his chalk in

1837, Falconer had served the parish no less than 47 years! One of his more noteworthy achievements appears to have been the stopping of the school's annual cockfight – a popular feature of any sporting curriculum at that time. As with Society schools, Bible knowledge was prominent on the parochial timetable. Latin was also a popular subject, along with some arithmetic, writing, grammar, a little geography and 'good manners'. Discipline of course was strict. Although all children were encouraged to attend, many families considered it worthwhile to enrol their sons only; hence the need for the more practically-orientated spinning schools for the daughters.

In 1855 a local benefactor, Colonel Campbell, offered to provide Ardclach parish with a third school. This was also to be in the north of the district, which the laird, Mr Brodie of Lethen, rightly deemed unnecessary, recognising a deficiency further inland. It was left to his neighbour, Lord Cawdor, to provide the site for the new school – at Achnatone only a mile from the existing Fornighty School. Nevertheless Campbell's School, as it came to be known, flourished.

At about this time, too. Lord Leven was establishing a small estate village (Ferness) on the opposite bank of the Findhorn from Ardclach itself. He included in the row of nine cottages a small school for his newly-housed tenants and employees. This private facility functioned for a short period only, however, because of a lack of suitable teachers.

The Education Act of 1872 did much to rationalise the complexities of private-, church- and Society-funded education. Most schools were accorded state assistance and were made accountable to a popularly-elected Board of local representatives. Religious instruction had to take second place to more secular pursuits and education became compulsory for all children aged between 5 and 13 (later raised to 14). It was this structural reorganisation which stimulated Robert Thomson to make the move from his Free Church post at Cawdor to the parish school at Ardclach.

By then Lord Leven's school at Ferness had closed, so the parochial institution at Ardclach enjoyed an extensive catchment from both sides of the Findhorn and further upstream as well. Local politics and rivalries strongly influenced policy and the newly-formed School Board had been able to provide Mr Brodie with a new building for Fornighty at a cost of £1500. This was only 50 yards from the boundary with Auldearn parish and a mile east of Campbell's School. It was not until 1888 that this obviously prejudiced School Board were finally voted out. The new members noted how their predecessors had been 'lavish in planting schools where they were not required' and lamented how the south side of the Findhorn lacked any provision at all now that the Ferness school had closed.

Admittedly Brodie had been conscious of this deficiency and, at his own expense, maintained a small school at Knockandhu, his game-keeper's house at Dunearn near Dulsie Bridge. This had been opened in 1883 with 15 pupils under Miss Caroline Murdoch, the daughter of a farmer nearby at Lynemore.

But the new School Board had other plans. Lord Leven offered them his empty school building at Ferness as a new parish school, there being too few families now in Ardclach itself to warrant a school on that side of the river. The sale of the old Ardclach building would then release funds enabling a new school to be built at Dulsie. Brodie, however, greatly resented these moves and responded by closing down his Knockandhu school altogether! Furthermore he was un-willing to permit the proposed Dulsie school to be built on his land. He was even more incensed when the School Board went on to suggest the closure of his Fornighty school in favour of Campbell's school. So he kept Fornighty open at his own expense and even canvassed the neighbouring districts for extra pupils until the roll was sufficient to qualify for state support! Much to his delight this created a new drain on the School Board's funds and necessitated their delaying the proposals for the new school at Dulsie. So in the meantime the Board had to be content with housing a temporary classroom in the farm of Burnside, not far from Knockandhu and Dulsie.

Eventually the Dulsie school problem came to be resolved, and in April 1893, 29 children entered a new building beside the picturesque and historic bridge of Dulsie. Even Mr Brodie had to approve, since many of the scholars were his tenants' children anyway. Indeed each summer Mrs Brodie generously treated the Dulsie pupils to a day's outing to Lethen House.

The transfer of the parish school from Ardclach to Ferness in 1889 had posed few problems. The old building was sold (to Mr Brodie, no less!) and the Thomson family took up residence in the refurbished schoolhouse in Ferness. As before, Elsie took charge of the infant class and Robert the seniors. Occasionally their daughter Elsie (who never married) would stand in for her mother or for the Dulsie teacher if either was ill.

In January 1882 Mrs Thomson began to keep a diary. Assistant teacher, busy housewife and mother, she was also a hard-working and much-respected member of the tight-knit rural community. She does not dwell on humdrum domestic details but instead portrays a vivid and sensitive picture of country life, personalities and events. The couple played an important part in parochial affairs and also con-tinued their natural history interests. The diary is punctuated with colourful descriptions of animals and the countryside, along with mention of many visitors, some of them very distinguished, such as the famous naturalist J.A. Harvie-Brown. Robert was much in demand to show off his extensive natural history collection, to give lectures and to lead field trips around local sites of historic interest.

Mrs Thomson was conscious of the decline in their little community. When she first moved into the area, Ardclach supported a population of about 1300 people. Old folk passed away and the youngsters moved on to other jobs, some of them abroad. By 1900 the parish contained fewer than 900 inhabitants. The Thomsons too had aged. In June 1900 an Inspector recorded in the Ferness School Log Book: 'Mrs Thomson, who used to assist in the school has been unwell for some time and unable to attend to the work. There is in consequence a falling off in the results and Mr Thomson himself has not the vigour of former times'.

The devoted couple finally retired in 1900, to their son's house in Uddingston near Glasgow. Mrs Thomson, long troubled with ill-health, died a year later. In his long widowhood, her husband Robert lovingly transcribed the diaries into two hard-covered notebooks in his neat and careful hand. He prefaced them with a detailed account of his own family background – a fascinating insight into life on an Aberdeenshire farm in the eighteenth century. Finally he added an account of his own upbringing and his first permanent teaching post in Cawdor. His son Robert, a much respected medical practitioner, died aged fifty in 1915, survived by his wife and a young daughter Helen. Robert senior lived for another eight years until 1923 when, aged 85, he too passed away.

The population of Ardclach is now less than 400. Dulsie school closed in 1951, Campbell's in 1960 and Fornighty ten years later. Ferness School, however, survives, with about a dozen pupils. Those from Dulsie have to be transported by car to Ferness. Children from the other schools' catchments are taken by bus to Auldearn or Nairn.

When Brenda became head teacher at Ferness in 1982, we moved into the schoolhouse already armed with a secondhand copy of a book by Robert Thomson entitled *The Natural History of a Highland Parish* – a work which had been written in that very house just before the old man had retired. We found the volume of tremendous interest and Brenda used it to good effect in a local history project with the children. Being a naturalist himself, John was intrigued by Robert Thomson and was eventually put in touch with his only surviving grandchild, Mrs Helen Lamb, daughter of the seventh and last Robert Thomson. Mrs Lamb generously let us see her grandfather's notebooks, and it is with her kind permission that we are able to edit and publish them.

Inverness Library and the local Education Office have permitted us to include extracts from the Ardclach and Ferness School Log Books. We have added a few relevant reports from the *Nairnshire Telegraph*, with kind agreement from the present Editor, Iain Bain, whose own great uncle published Robert Thomson's book. Finally we should like to thank Mr Ewen Brodie of Lethen, Mr and Mrs F. Masson, and Mr and Mrs W. Macleod for allowing us to reproduce photographs of times past. The remaining photos and line drawings are by John Love.

John Love and Brenda McMullen

CHAPTER I

Tenant at Todlochy

My father, Robert Thomson – the fifth, so far as he could trace, of the same christian name – was born in the year 1765 at Todlochy, a small farm of about seventy acres on the estate of Sir Archibald Grant, Baronet of Monymusk. Of the various events of his life I retain only fragmentary recollections as communicated to me by my mother, and these are often dissociated from date and locality. There is, however, no reason to suppose that his experience differed in any material respect from that of other boys whose lot had been cast in similar circumstances.

His memory went back to an early period and one incident, trivial as it may seem, appears to have deeply impressed itself on his young mind. When some four or five years of age, his mother in the hope of conferring a real pleasure, gave him a new bonnet and promised to take him to the church on the next Sunday. The day came, but after being fittingly attired he refused to put on the cap, insisting that he liked the old one better. In deference, however, to a higher authority he ultimately had to yield, but continued peevish and fretful as they trudged along the road. Having to cross a brattling stream in full flood, he quickly seized the opportunity and with great delight sent the despised head-dress floating down the current – never, he hoped, to worry him any more.

He could easily trace the four consecutive generations who had held the tenancy of the farm previous to his time, but how many of his forefathers in earlier years had lived and died in Todlochy? Tradition herself failed to give even a hazy account. The family burying ground in the parish church-yard consisted of three adjacent lairs with one central headstone erected during his own life . . .

When a breach in the family circle rendered it necessary to open a grave, my father often took a mournful interest on the funeral day, in trying to identify the osseous fragments of deceased relatives as the parts were thrown up by the sexton or lay exposed to view upon the loose earth. The Thomsons, he said, had always been greatly respected in the district and were noted for much kindliness of heart, as manifested in a generous hospitality to the local poor, as well as not a few homeless wanderers who were never allowed to go empty from the door.

When not much turned of seventeen, the subject of this narrative, though physically immature and with little or no experience of the outside world had, along with his sister Ann, to undertake the complete management of the holding owing to straitened circumstances and the failing ability of their two aged parents. Agriculture about the end of the eighteenth century, being still prosecuted in the parish, as elsewhere, on the old fashioned lines, was seldom the means of providing the farmer with many of the luxuries of this life. Even after much hard toil in the spring months, the harvests often turned out almost a total failure, on account of untimely rain or blighting frosts towards the end of the season. As nearly one half of the rent had to be paid at the mansion-house in grain, the family at times had to practise the greatest economy with respect to the scanty remainder, if any . . .

The farmer had his cattle and perhaps a few sheep to supply him with at least food and raiment. Then, too, the sale of his young stock in the neighbouring markets generally enabled him to settle with the landlord and occasionally procure a few things greatly needed for the comfort of his family. With the view of reducing their expenditure to a minimum, the brother and sister with the assistance of a herd-boy, struggled for some years to do all the field and dairywork. Throughout the winter and spring months my father rose in the mornings long before dawn, and in the dim light of a moss-fir taper stuck in the barn wall, he thrashed with the flail the straw which was necessary to feed the cattle during the day. When the weather at all permitted, after the usual breakfast of porridge and milk about eight o'clock, he went out and followed the plough till darkness set in after sunset. His dinner and fresh oxen were regularly brought to the field by his sister, that the work might be delayed as little as possible before the winter storms came on. Thus it sometimes happened that – Sunday excepted – he seldom saw the inside of his own house with daylight for weeks on end.

The corn-crops had been often poor, but the yield in 1782 was specially disappointing. As the Todlochy harvest in that year produced only nine pecks of standard grain, my father had to face one of the severest trials of his life. With such a scanty return it was quite impossible to pay the rent and provide for the domestic wants in the home. Fitting himself, therefore, to the sad conditions of the case, he determined to apply for outside employment, and at the same time attend to his own private concerns as best he could.

Fortunately the Commissioners for the county of Aberdeen were engaged in building a turnpike road from the city to the Highland border on the West. A great number of farmers, my father amongst them, were only too glad to enter the service. Naturally the contractors took advantage of the glut in the labour market and attended severely to their own interests. Arranging to pay their men every night, they noted those whom they considered inefficient or slow at work during the day, and the gaffer, in handing them their wages said, 'Your Place has been filled by another, and you are no longer required'. Not a few heard this announcement as if it had been a judicial sentence condemning them to a period of penal servitude. To avoid such a misfortune my father exerted himself to the utmost with pick, barrow and spade, and often related in after life that, when he came home tired and weary with the day's work, his hands felt hot and throbbed as if an unhappy heart had been beating in every finger. At night too, a series of cold chills often ran through his feverish frame, like so many electric currents, and disturbed his sleep. Although he always looked forward in dread to the pay-hour, his dark forebodings were never realized.

The work, in that district, was continued for several months and in the end he took his own discharge, having earned a sum sufficient to provide for the family needs, and at the same time liquidate all his current liabilities. Thus he learned that honest labour imparted a self-reliant spirit which fits the toiler to occupy an honourable place in society. The hard experience proved of the greatest value to him and in due course he became a sober upright young man.

As agriculture was then beginning to be conducted on greatly improved principles, Todlochy never again produced such a miserable crop. Two years later there was, strange to say, an abundant harvest all over the country and the people in their gratitude, unwilling that it should be forgotten, endeavoured to perpetuate the welcome boon in the simple couplet: -

'Seventeen hundred and eighty four
Caused all our girnals to run o'er.'

From that time the tide of prosperity set in and continued to flow until my father found himself in easy circumstances, and had it not been for a very liberal hospitality and a generous kindness to his less fortunate neighbours, he might have attained even to comparative affluence.

In the course of nature my paternal grandfather – the fourth Robert Thomson – died at the age of seventy three and his spouse some twenty years later at eighty eight. Not long after their only daughter, Ann, followed and was laid beside her parents in the quiet churchyard of Monymusk. Her brother being now left alone decided to marry Sarah Simpson, a woman of much native sagacity, with a great amount of buoyant humour, but whose kindly nature was so fully in sympathy with her husband's that it was a source of wonder to many how the limited supplies of so small a farm could stand the constant drain to which it was subjected, but then we are told, 'there is that scattereth and yet increaseth'.

In the immediate vicinity of the farm house under the shade of a few ash trees, which in their venerable massiveness spoke of bygone centuries, there stood six or eight old-fashioned low-browed huts. These were built of turf and rough hill stones in alternate layers, while the roofs were thatched with straw and roped diagonally after the manner of a hay stack. The tiny hamlet presented somewhat the appearance of huge bee-hives set down in the leafy shade without the least attempt at order or effect. In these lived my father's cottars – a partial survival of a system of land-tenure once very common in Scotland. These, as required, worked upon the farm and depended upon him for a great part of their daily bread.

To the local vagrants, of whom there were many, Todlochy was well known. When strolling about over the district they seldom failed to make a call, knowing from past experience that they would not be turned away without a substantial dole. Three families in particular, with a good deal of gipsy blood in them – Napiers, Neds and Raphaels – believing that they had acquired a prescriptive right to 'quarters' if they cared to avail themselves of it, sometimes stayed for several days on end. Accordingly, a few old blankets patched and darned till it was difficult to distinguish the original fabric, were kept in the barn for their special benefit. Then at night the individual members, with these coverings thrown over, crawled under a heap of loose straw and often slept as soundly as any of the better class did on their more luxurious beds of feathers or down. During the day these beggars were exceedingly troublesome to the farmer's wife, being continually in want of 'a spoonful' of milk, of 'a wee bit' of bread or butter to supplement a jolly feast on some unlucky fowl struck down in middle life, or hapless hare destroyed without a game licence, together with many untimely conveniences when the domestics were busy with their own household duties in the kitchen.

As the manufacture of horn-spoons, tin basins and pitchers was their chief business, they, at times, nominally without charge, executed any odd repairs in connection with these articles or other cooking utensils belonging to the family. In pursuit of their precarious vocation they travelled over large areas in the northern counties, and in the absence of the modern newspaper, were the accredited retailers of much general and political gossip among the humbler peasantry. Although gross lying, without a moral sense, was an acknowledged trait of their character, their chatter was eagerly listened to by the simple rustics who stared in wonder at the strange stories they had to tell of men and things in other parts of the country. Even the children could lisp in fiction and were always delighted to get one or more of the cottars to attend to their little tale.

. . . In the faithful discharge of her voluntary duties [Mrs Thomson] unfortunately caught infection which in due course, developed and carried her away after a short illness. Then amid general sorrow, my father laid her remains to rest among his ancestral dust in the quiet church-yard of Monymusk.

The deceased goodwife was the mother of three children – Robert, a very thoughtful and promising boy who passed away after a short illness, at the age of thirteen, from the effects of a snow-ball which struck him on the ear; Sarah, who was spared only for a few months, and Mary, who alone reached the years of maturity. She was a kindly gentle girl and, being endowed with a bright and winning manner, soon became a great favourite in the community. Tall and comely in person, with fair hair and light blue eyes which sparkled like stars in her clear waxen complexion, she was reputed to be, in her day, the handsomest maiden in the parish. Her first sweetheart – a lad of considerable talent – sent her a very beautiful valentine which I have carefully preserved. It was designed, drawn and coloured by himself, but for some unknown reason their courtship was broken off, and she ultimately decided to cast in her lot with that of a rival admirer, Andrew Wyse by name. Dying at the age of twenty six, she left four children but as their father removed to a distant part of the country before my day, none of them ever came within the circle of my friends or acquaintances.

My father was born too far back in the eighteenth century to have, in his station, much attention paid to his education. When a boy about to enter his teens, he was sent to the parish school but had to leave at the end of six weeks and return to his usual duties on the farm. Nevertheless, he could read and write fairly well and had some knowledge even of arithmetic. Through life, he always perused with pleasure and often profit, any book on suitable subjects that he chanced to fall in with, though it could not be said that he was by any means extensively read. Endowed, however, with considerable mental power, together with a keen observant faculty, he readily embraced every opportunity for improvement, especially in things relating to husbandry. Nor, though this talent had been but little cultivated, was he devoid of an eye for appreciating both the beautiful and curious in Nature.

As a man of genuine integrity, he was much respected and often consulted by friends and neighbours regarding their more important transactions. In carrying on his own business, I never heard that he incurred a single pecuniary obligation which he had not ready cash to discharge. Not only, in his day, was he an up to date farmer but also a shrewd operative mechanic who was generally able to construct and repair his own agricultural implements as well as most articles of household furniture. In these circumstances he should have had little difficulty in acquiring a competency for his old age but, his ear being ever open to the local tales of poverty and misfortune, he practised economy for the pleasure of helping those whom he believed to be in need. Now and again he advanced money on loan but as this was invariably done by verbal agreement, only a very few remembered the date on which they had promised to repay the amount due.

During one season, as the result of a cattle disease, he lost considerably over one hundred pounds. This was a severe blow and reduced the family to the greatest straits. In course of time however, prosperity returned and continued to flow till the end of his lease, thus enabling him to wipe out all his arrears and leave a good credit balance at the bank. For many years he devoted a great deal of attention to apiculture and kept such a stock of bees in the garden that he sometimes sold honey enough to pay the money part of his Martinmas rent.

My father was quite turned of three score and ten years when he decided to marry for the second time. His future wife, Mary Urquhart, was then in domestic service some four miles from Todlochy with a bachelor master who had been making advances to her with a view to a closer relationship. She did not feel able to respond so he changed his tactics towards her and adopted a policy of petty annoyances as opportunity presented itself. Desertion in those days was seldom thought of and she accordingly resolved to put up with the crook in her lot till the following term. This experience was not a little trying, as in her former situation she had the happy fortune to be received into the family as an adopted daughter. This relationship continued with Mr Alexander Reid and his wife Jane until it was finally dissolved in the course of Nature by the death of her two beloved friends.

In the following summer, she had occasion to visit her parents at the Braes of Kincardine O'Niel and, while on the way chanced to pass my father and another man cutting peat by the roadside. The house-dog, a fine collie, was lying on the sward and keeping watch close by. As she approached, he looked up and gave a low growl, which she mistook for a canine warning to take care. 'Come away', said the man on the bank, 'there's no fear of you; he's a good natured beast, and won't bite.' Then turning haply aside for a minute or so to pat him in a friendly way, the three entered into a short bantering conversation – the man in 'the stank' however, only occasionally putting in a word. By and bye the chief speaker remarked that she was a good looking damsel and told her that his companion was sorely in need of a sensible wife and that he would make an excellent husband for her. Treating the whole affair as a piece of good-humoured pleasantry she continued the jocularity for a short time longer and then, bidding them farewell, thought no more about her casual meeting with the way-side strangers. In our family this simple occurrence was destined to be productive of very important results and, to judge from present appearances, may continue even far into the future.

Not long afterwards, when my father, in Sunday attire, paid her an unlooked-for visit in the 'gloaming,' she failed for a little to remember where she had seen him. A reference, however, to the moss incident recalled their former meeting and they spent some time in pleasant conversation about things in general. All the while she could not think what his reason for seeing her might be. In due course his real object began to dawn upon her. His proposal to espouse her in marriage came as a great surprise but, after a little consideration, she made up her mind and firmly declined. Her admirer, though seemingly disappointed, took the matter calmly and, after continuing the interview for a few minutes longer, set out on his way home, some four miles distant.

In the weeks that followed, my mother's domestic troubles rather increased and on due reflection, she came to the conclusion that she had lightly thrown away perhaps the last chance she might ever get of happily settling her lot in life. By a strange Providence, however, my father returned soon after, renewed his offer and was accepted. Without delay everything was arranged and the union took place as in the following newspaper announcement: –

> '*At Tillyfroe, Cluny, Aberdeenshire, on the 1st of September 1836, by the Rev James Paterson, M.A., United Presbyterian Church, Midmar, Robert Thomson, Farmer, Todlochy, Monymusk, to Mary, third daughter of Alexander Urquhart, Farmer, Wester Tolmads, Kincardine O'Neill.*'

There was a considerable disparity between their ages. He was seventy one and she was scarcely turned of thirty six, but the relation proved in every respect a thoroughly satisfactory one. My mother was honest, open of heart and brought a savour of sincere piety into her new home. Strange to say, though she lived in an age which was darkened with the cramping fogs of superstition, I never heard her express the slightest belief in ghosts, witches, water kelpies or such like occult agencies. With the Bible narrative she was quite familiar and in early life had committed to memory the Psalms of David, as well as the whole of the Larger and Shorter Catechisms together with the relative Scriptural proofs. At a later period she took a great interest in religious literature. Her favourite authors, whose works she had read over and over again, were Milton's 'Paradise Lost'; Young's 'Night Thoughts'; Pollock's 'Course of Time', and Hervey's 'Meditations'. Next year, I was born on the tenth of August and my brother Alexander on the tenth of April 1839, but he only survived till the twenty fourth of July following.

The leases on the Monymusk estate expired soon after and, the proprietor having announced that he would decline a renewal to any tenant who was advanced in life, my father had to seek for another home. Very fortunately a small holding, in the parish of Nigg, Kincardineshire, at a nominal rent with a tenure of some fifty years, came into the market and was secured for a reasonable amount. The previous owner, being a man of considerable refinement, had laid out the whole place with great taste and skill. Two years later, the subject of this narrative was laid aside from an internal tumour which carried him away on the 31st January 1841 at the ripe age of seventy six, and my mother with her little boy was left alone. Thenceforth she had to face life on the produce of her twelve acres and the sum of £200 at her credit in the bank. Finding that the land in her hands was unprofitable, she decided to sell off and build two dwelling houses at Charleston on the neighbouring property.

Then, after a widowhood of nine years, she entered into a second marriage on the 24th of October 1850. Her husband, Donald MacKeddie, a native of Cromarty, had served in the Royal Navy under Sir Charles Napier and was retired as a Greenwich out-pensioner. Considering his life's experience at sea, he had great respect for everything sacred and, as he said, 'having fought for freedom' at once cast in his lot with the Free Church. He was a strong supporter of Disruption principles and, through his enthusiasm, both his wife and the writer became at an early period sympathetic members of the dissenting body. Family worship he kept twice a day, was hospitable to friends and straightforward in every transaction. Neither in ordinary conversation nor when ruffled in temper did he ever use a strong word – his yea was yea, and his nay, nay. At the ripe age of seventy six he died, on the 29th of June 1860, and his remains were interred in the Free Church grave-yard at Banchory Devenick. A little later my mother came to reside with us in the Free Church Schoolhouse, Cawdor where she died on the 15th of September 1870 in the seventieth year of her age, and was laid to rest in the parish Churchyard there. She left for us a note which read.

Dear son, I die, but God shall be with you. Dear Elsie, I have been very earnest for a blessing on you and my son together, and I leave you both upon Him by faith . . .'

Regarding the life of my maternal grandfather, Alexander Urquhart, Farmer, Wester Tolmads, Kincardine O'Neill, there is not much that can now be written. He was the youngest, and only boy in a family of six. During childhood, he showed signs of a weakly constitution, which along with a decided myopic vision led his parents to think of educating him for the ministry – a course which would have been alike suitable to his inclinations and capacities.

While at school he made rapid progress, but when about to enter the University, both parents died within a short time of each other, and left him to struggle on the small farm for the support of his five sisters. Although his professional career was thus cut short, the taste for literature remained, and proved a source of much real pleasure to him throughout a long life. He possessed a fairly good collection of books, chiefly of a religious kind, and these he had read over and over again. With the Sacred Scriptures he was thoroughly familiar from Genesis to Revelations and, at an early age, had committed to memory the Psalms of David, as well as a great many favourite chapters in the Old and New Testaments. When quite a young man he was elected an elder of the local Session Church, and there were few of his associates whose Christian faith and piety were more intense and sincere. In the discharge of his official duties he did what he could for the education of the rising generation but, strange to say, did not approve of girls being taught to write in case they might be tempted to engage in frivolous correspondence with their sweethearts! At family worship the good man, in the absence of a candle, frequently repeated a suitable chapter and psalm, while the concluding prayer on behalf of himself and kneeling forms, was an exercise of great solemnity and fervour. But like the Psalmist he could say:

Seven times a day it is my care
To give due praise to thee.

The dwelling house occupied the central position in a long line of farm offices – byre, barn, stable etc – and consisted of a low dingy erection of turf and hill stones in alternate layers, with four or five rooms all on the ground floor. As the seasons waned and the evenings closed in, the various cottars living near by often gathered in considerable numbers to spend the forenight round his big ha' fire. Then while the shadowy light from the glowing peat fell with uncertain glimmer upon the dark walls and smoke-blackened rafters, the visitors employed the passing hours by discussing second-hand politics, narrating some stirring tale or exciting legend of bygone times.

In due course my grandfather married bonny Mary, the eldest daughter of John Anderson, farmer, Broom Fould in the neighbourhood. The issue of this union was a family of one son and six daughters, who all lived to have homes of their own. Between the decease of his parents and the first break in his happy circle there elapsed a period of fifty years, which led him sometimes to remark that Death had surely forgotten to knock at the door of his humble abode. His wife proved a great blessing to him in many respects. Gifted with a genial personality which endeared her to everyone, she kept her sweet and winsome manner throughout a long life. She discharged her domestic duties with great tact and economy till the last hour when heart and flesh began to fail in August 1854, and she passed away at the ripe age of ninety six.

Throughout the eighteenth century, agriculture continued in a very backward condition, and the frequent failure of the grain crops, from summer drought or autumn frosts, was the cause of much trouble and even privation to many a poor farmer. The individual experiences of 'bad years' often formed the subject of doleful conversation during the long winter evenings as they sat round the glowing fire in the cosy cottage of some popular neighbour. On one occasion, my grandfather, under the pressure of hard times, was reduced almost to the verge of bankruptcy and, in his distress, was seriously considering the propriety of selling out and trying his fortune in the New World. His wife however, who was greatly averse to any such wild project, laid before him the Scripture passage, 'Trust in the Lord and do good, so shalt thou dwell in the land, and verily thou shalt be fed'. After considering the matter, to her extreme delight, he agreed to remain at home and it turned out as she fully expected. In the following years the tide of prosperity began to flow, and they soon found themselves in easy circumstances.

As the good man advanced in life his strength began to fail, and a cancerous growth took root on his right shoulder. Before setting out for a medical operation in Aberdeen, he called in four of his esteemed friends and, having settled some family affairs, he arranged with them to take charge of his coffin at the churchyard and lower it into the grave. When the end came the funeral took place on a beautiful day in June 1842, and the remains were laid to rest in the old burying ground of Tough, till the last trump shall sound on the morning of the great and final day.

CHAPTER 2

A Loon at Large

One fine summer day towards the end of July, when a boy between ten and twelve years of age, I was playing with a favourite companion beside a deep pool whose surface, I should think, would not be more than some eight or ten square yards. By and by, we became deeply interested in sailing a tiny boat from side to side. All went well till, on reaching too far over the edge to direct its course, I lost my balance and fell in. Believing, as I sank to the bottom, that my end had come, I folded my hands and made no effort to regain the bank. Fortunately, however, my young friend was equal to the occasion, and pulled me out whenever my body appeared above the water. As the sun was riding high in a cloudless sky the day was very warm, and so we both agreed to search for blaeberries on the moor till my clothes became sufficiently dry to arouse no suspicion as to what had happened on my return home.

A year or two later, a few of the bigger boys and myself who were attending the parish school arranged one Saturday to go down, during the usual half holiday, to the sea-shore at the Cove near Aberdeen and spend some hours on the dry tract laid bare by the ebb between the tide marks in pursuit of limpets *Patella vulgaris*; the edible periwinkle *Littorina littorea*; together with dulse *Rhodymenia palmata* and other members of the Algae family. For a time, we all enjoyed ourselves to the full and found much to wonder at as we cautiously scrambled over the slippery crags which had been recently uncovered by the great ocean in front. By and by three lads, unknown to me, appeared over the brow of the 'heugh' which rose sheer up to the height of nearly three hundred feet from close on the water's edge, and began to throw stones at us for mere amusement. Very soon, as it happened, I was struck on the side of the head just above the right eye and immediately fell stunned to the ground. My companions did the little best they could to restore consciousness and stop the bleeding. After a time they were successful and helped me home with great care. Strange to say, the wound healed with the first intention but the scar remains to this day, quite evident to the touch, though there was no disfigurement of the part.

From earliest childhood I was taught by my mother that swearing, even in the most modified forms, was sinful, being at all times needless and morally degrading. 'Fegs and Heth, Losh and Gosh' though common in conversation, she impressed upon me were simply 'minced oaths' and therefore to be absolutely avoided. Referring to the highest authority, she said, 'Let your yea be yea, and your nay, nay, for whatsoever is more than these cometh of evil'. Although many of my companions indulged very freely in this vulgar depravity, I never cared to follow their example until I was a boy of about twelve years of age. One day thinking over this habit, I decided to show off my little manliness on the first suitable opportunity by using some of the strongest expletives which I had heard from the farmers and their men servants when angry. Accordingly, not long after, when engaged in some rough play with five or six boys like myself, I chanced to break an important rule of the game and was thrown down to receive condign punishment. Thereupon I forthwith broke out and swore like a dragoon. The effect was truly magical. My chums, who had never heard me use a 'bad' word before, were astounded and I myself felt greatly ashamed. In consequence, the sport at once ceased and all, under a sense of wrong doing, gradually separated and slunk away quietly home. From that day forward I never again had the least desire to emphasise even my severest remarks in any words other than the purest at my command, and on all occasions found that they fully served my purposes both with dignity and effect.

Having made up my mind after some hesitation, to adopt the teaching profession, I went south in 1854 and entered the Glasgow Free Church Normal College where I remained for two years. Here I got bursaries worth £25 which, with considerable help from home, enabled me to procure not a few comforts which were denied to some of my fellow students . . .

. . . Not long after my arrival in the great city, a favourite comrade and I, after some serious conversation on the subject, agreed to pay a visit to the Royal Theatre, in order to witness the popular play of the Battle of Alma fought in the Crimea, on the 20th of September 1854, between the allied forces of Great Britain and France, and the Russians, but the histrionic talent of the company did not come up to my expectations. The pictorial features, though good enough of their kind, had a very different effect upon me from the one it had been intended to produce. The painted canvas and the obvious acting served to show that we were simply in a theatre and merely viewing a dramatic performance. When the whole was finished, I thought that the price to be paid in time and money for such an artificial representation was too high seeing that, if so minded, I could read and enjoy the whole story fully as well in my own room at home. Thus the temptation of play-going in after life was never sufficiently strong to induce me to return more than two or three times at long intervals, and even on these occasions it was in each case to gratify the desire of some special friend.

In due course, I left the Normal [College] and on the 10th of August 1856, my twentieth birthday, I commenced professional duty as *locum tenens* for a few months in the Free Church School, Newhills, near Aberdeen. Two of the scholars, a boy and a girl, aged some eight and six years respectively, greatly interested me as they had been slaves for nearly six months in the southern States of America. Their mother was the daughter of a very respectable family in the neighbourhood. Soon after her marriage, which was not a happy one, she and her husband emigrated to New York, where the children were born. By and by, the father deserted and left his wife to struggle for herself and family as best she could. In her dire distress, the poor woman sold her offspring into bondage and disappeared among the back woods of the country. When the grandmother heard the sad news, she crossed the Atlantic and redeemed the hapless little ones at great cost.

One morning after having heard the infants their lesson, wee Maggie placed herself between my knees, as I sat on a chair in the classroom and, looking kindly up in my face said, 'Are you married?' Not a little surprised at such a question I replied in the negative. 'Well then', she added, 'Would you take our Ellen?' After a short pause I asked, 'Is she a nice lassie? Tell her to come up some day and see me'. On returning to my rooms in the evening I related the incident to Mrs Nicolson and inquired, 'Who is Ellen?' 'Oh, she is the youngest daughter of the family, and is a bright and dashing girl'. An hour later my landlady called me from the tea-table saying, 'Here is your admirer passing along the street. Come and you will get a glimpse of her'. On looking out at the window, our eyes instantly met. The shock was too much for me, and I took refuge behind the curtain. Next morning our little ambassadress, before returning to her usual seat in school came up to me and, laying her chubby hand in mine said, 'Why did you go back from the window when our Ellen looked up to you last night?' 'Ah', I replied, 'tell Ellen that she's a very pretty girl and that I hope to meet her soon.' This, however, was not to be, as I had to leave in a few days after for an appointment at Bourtreebush in Kincardine.

During the following summer the woods and moorland slopes along the coast furnished me, after school hours, with very congenial recreation. I began to make a collection of the local insects and to study their nature and habits, both for personal and professional benefit. At an early stage, the Diadem Spider *Epeira diadema*, which constructs its wonderful net so artistically between two trees or in any other suitable opening, soon became a special favourite. When examining the webs and gossamer threads, so often seen on a dewy morning in autumn spread over the whole face of the ground, I could not help admiring the skill and inherent aptitude of the whole race.

Among its associated tribes were the splendid dragon-flies, the crimson-spotted Burnet moths and particularly the small blue and red butterflies. While searching one day at the foot of the beetling cliffs on the sea-shore, I found the rare Brown Argus *Lycaena artaxerxes*, in considerable numbers sporting about like moving flakes of colour in the bright sunshine and occasionally resting on the blossoms of the ragweed to sip the nectar contained in the floral cups. Like others in this gorgeous family, they are delicate creatures but possessed of the distinctive discoidal white spot on each of their sepia-brown wings, which renders them the envy of the entomologist to fill what is so often an empty space in his cabinet.

Proud of my discovery, I somewhat rashly inserted an intimation in one of the Natural History papers that I would be glad to give specimens in exchange for any others from the south. To my surprise, for the next two weeks, insects in great numbers were sent to me on trust for as many of this scarce variety as I could give. In all I received one hundred and fifty letters – not a few being from members of families with good positions both in the Church and State. My landlady could not understand what had come about to account for such an extraordinary correspondence but the local postrunner, confident of the true solution, tried to relieve her anxiety by stating that the young schoolmaster had just fallen heir to a valuable estate. The task of collecting and preparing the necessary specimens was very great. In the circumstances I did the best possible but often regretted that I failed, for lack of the 'flying stock', to carry out my good intentions.

The wild bees too, on account of their astonishing intelligence and social life, had peculiar charms for me. There was the common Foggie-bee *Bombus muscorum* which looks out for a slight depression in the surface and then erects over it a dome of moss to shelter and conceal its honey-jars. Another was the courageous Red-backed bee *Bombus lapidarius* whose underground homestead, I well remembered from early experience, could scarcely be outraged with impunity. Then I was greatly struck with the artful policy of the aristocratic *Apathus vestalis*, who so fully resembles its host, the

Scotch Argus

Bombus terrestris, that it not only enters the nest without molestation but lives on friendly terms with the owners, feeding on the common stores and even rears its young side by side in the general nursery. Little doubt however, it does perform in the community some important office, the nature of which it would be interesting to find out. Not less worthy of notice was the Tree-wasp, whose papery mansion is so delicately and beautifully made. In spite of its material and structure it is perfectly able to resist the ordinary storms of both wind and rain.

Next year (1858) in the course of the autumn holidays I answered two advertisements in the *Witness* newspaper for a teacher – the one in the Presbytery of Fordoun and the other in Nairnshire. The correspondent of the former, I thought, was somewhat long in replying. By and by however, a misaddressed letter reached me, more than three weeks after its date and bore on the envelope the stamps of a dozen different post offices.

Trivial as such an occurrence may appear in the light of a not infrequent experience, it was the means of entirely altering the whole sequence of my future life. But so far as I am now able to judge I have never had the least reason to regret it. The writer stated that I had been chosen master of the particular school and requested me to come on as soon as possible. Taking the first train to the south, I duly arrived at Mills of Kincardine and found the farmer at home. In the mutual explanations which followed, he informed me that as no reply had been received to the missive sent, his colleagues at their next meeting resolved to offer the situation to the second gentleman on the list and, as everything had been satisfactorily arranged they expected him to commence duties at once.

CHAPTER 3

A Class at Cawdor

A day or two afterwards the postman handed me a communication from the Rev. S.F. Maclauchlan announcing that the Cawdor Free Church managers had elected me to fill the vacancy in their congregational school which he hoped I would be able to reopen just after the holidays. Pleased with the prospect, I arrived on the 24th of October 1858 and among the first scholars whose names I entered on the register were two boys, William Cameron, now chief Constable of Partick, and James MacKenzie, for many years Manager of a large wood merchant's business in Glasgow.

The minister gave me every encouragement and the parishioners generally appeared greatly interested when they came to know of my Natural History propensities. It was evident from the flora of the district that it would prove a rich field for the Entomologist and I employed my leisure hours to great profit in searching the pine and oak woods for the living treasures which they contained. The Northern Brown butterfly *Erebia blandina* occurred in great numbers but strange to say is seldom found along the sea-board to the west of Forres.

In April 1860 I was asked to spend a Saturday at Cawdor Castle and dined in the evening with Mr Stables who was himself greatly interested in the Botany and Geology of the Old Province of Moray. After an excellent dinner my friend suggested a glass of toddy to which I agreed, though entirely out of deference to the desire of my host. That finished, he insisted on a second and, as my will-power in those days was rather weak in the presence of superiors, I reluctantly consented. Thereafter we retired to the library to inspect his Herbarium and the other objects of interest. As he opened out the various packets I found that the dried specimens were dancing before my eyes and that I could not, save with some difficulty, read their scientific names. The state into which I had unwittingly brought myself was to be much regretted and, though my condition could not be considered a favourable one for making a resolution, I determined from that moment never again to sacrifice my mental powers at the shrine of any drinking usage, and through life, although not a strict total abstainer, I have been enabled scrupulously to adhere to my vow.

The butterflies, being sun-loving creatures, were comparatively easy of capture and it was not long till all the local kinds were represented in my collection. As the moths, however, have considerable wing power and nearly always fly in the twilight or during the darkness of night I had, like other Entomologists, to adopt various plans in order to secure those nocturnal beauties. Gradually the drawers in my cabinet were being filled up and even contained a few species seldom to be found elsewhere. About this time the Rev. George Gordon Birnie, near Elgin, observing my name in a Natural History paper as a working amateur in the district, began a correspondence with me in the hope of being able to supplement his own List of the Lepidoptera which he was compiling for the Old Province of Moray. In furtherance of this object I was desired to send my insects to the manse so as to have the various sorts taken in Cawdor noted and their nomenclature confirmed by actual inspection. He examined and compared my specimens with great interest and thereafter I had the pleasure of spending two days in his company, while visiting the ruined 'Lanthorn of the North' [Elgin Cathedral].

We talked over its chequered history, and especially its heartless destruction by the Wolf of Badenoch in 1390. On that occasion the vesper hymn had scarcely died away through the long aisles when a body of horsemen, under the Earl from Lochindorbh, entered the town from the west. Almost before the burghers were aware the splendid edifice was seen to be illuminated through all the rich tracery of its Gothic windows, by a furious fire which raged within. Far and wide, tower and spire blazed like gigantic torches and, bathed in flame, glared out against a background of darkness to form one of the most picturesque scenes which anyone could witness. It was an act of sheeer vandalism for which the noble culprit had to go through the most humiliating penance before Bishop Barr would agree to absolve his guilt, and again receive him within the pale of the Holy Mother Church.

After giving the 'Harvest Play' in August 1861, I was asked by an upland farmer to spend a week at his place in the Streens, one of the most picturesque straths along the Findhorn. While sauntering for

Elgin Cathedral

some miles by the winding stream, I found myself almost entirely shut out from the face of Nature. On each side the ravine is flanked by a massive wall of metamorphic rock which rises wild and rugged for several hundreds of feet from the intervening flat. In consequence a few cottages on the right bank are completely cut off from the rays of the noonday sun for nearly three weeks before and after the winter solstice.

Curious to explore a new locality, I next day ascended the hill behind the farm house and, from a lofty peak, gazed on a wide expanse of country which spread out all round to the far horizon, with the clear blue sky arching as an immense dome over the whole. To the north the eye could dimly see the Ord of Caithness with the hills of Sutherland and Ross, while Ben Wyvis, the Moray Firth and a large stretch of Nairnshire lay about half way between. Turning to the south I beheld, in billowy undulations, an unbroken tract of heathery moors which, fringed by the snow-capped Grampian range, gave dignity and power to the awe-inspiring scene. Here and there, the surface was relieved by the soft verdure of a distant croft while all over it was irregularly seamed and mottled with river, lake or mossy tarn. Such a magnificent view indelibly impressed on my mind the picture of a broad and varied landscape which was only once again equalled when I stood on the summit of Ben Wyvis in September 1867.

About a mile from the farm house, in a lovely cottage by the river side, there lived a single, middle-aged spinster who earned a precarious livelihood during the spring and summer months as a fieldworker. To eke out a scanty income she kept a large flock of hens which, at the time of my visit, were being allowed to feed without restraint among the farmer's lea oats at the end of her house. Taking down his gun one morning after breakfast, my host announced to me with some warmth that he had made up his mind to shoot every one of the depredators, and asked if I cared to accompany him on his punitive mission. Desirous to see this kind of doubtful sport, I at once agreed, and so we both set out for the scene of operations. On our arrival the whole poultry tribe, as we expected, were holding high revel in the midst of a fine crop, and had evidently picked the grain and trampled down the straw over a considerable area. Just as the farmer was raising the gun to his shoulder I said, 'As the hens are to be killed, perhaps you would allow me to fire the shot?' Most certainly,' he replied, 'and I'll stand between you and all danger.' Accordingly I took the fowling piece, pointed it in the proper direction, closed my eyes and drew the trigger. Hearing a loud report, the poor woman guessed the reason, and came out to see what had actually happened. Becoming greatly excited, she delivered herself in forcible Gaelic as to the character of the person who could be guilty of such a deed. On me, however, her tirade had no effect, as I knew only one word – schoolmaster.

About three weeks afterwards I received a letter from her law agent in Nairn stating that I had killed a very fine cock, valued at a guinea, together with thirteen hens, for all of which his client demanded the sum of one pound ten shillings. Soon after I called on the writer who was not a little amused at my case, but advised me to settle the matter by private agreement. Taking his advice, I asked a decent neighbour to visit the old lady and on my behalf to obtain from her the best terms possible. This he did, and paid her the sum of thirteen shillings! The lesson was a wholesome one and although my friends often complimented me as a crack shot, it was, I am pleased to add, the first and only time I ever fired a gun with intent to kill.

. . . In the spring of 1862, one of the Castle servants, while ploughing on the home farm, came upon a prehistoric grave at Tomnahooly, some twelve inches below the surface. As usual this last resting place was formed by placing four unhewn slabs on their edges with a larger one atop to protect the remains. Inside it contained a complete skeleton of a man in fairly good condition together with a rudely ornamented clay urn, now in the Nairn museum. Close by had been laid the deceased's personal javelin and harpoon, the spear-shaped bone points of which resisted decay. Next day I found, among the loose earth, a similar weapon, but in chisel form and carefully polished, no doubt to answer a particular purpose. Some time afterwards when talking to Mr Stables on the subject, he told me that it was very rare and asked if I would part with it to the British Museum, and that the thanks of the trustees, along with a drawing of the same, would be sent to me in due course. This was done; but the acknowledgement having been apparently drawn out in his Lordship's name, it never reached me. During the summer of 1907, however, when spending an hour or two in the Antiquarian Museum, Edinburgh, I observed a bone in one of the prehistoric cases very like the above. As it bore to have been originally given by the Earl of Cawdor to the British Museum and thereafter handed over to the Scottish institution, I felt confident that it was the very relic discovered many years previously by myself.

A few weeks after my appointment in Cawdor I happened to call at Meikle Geddes and was kindly received by Mrs Fraser, the farmer's widowed sister. While talking together in the parlour, Elsie, her only daughter, came tripping into the room – no doubt curious to see the young schoolmaster – and took an intelligent part in our general conversation. Her frank and winsome manner, graceful figure and sweet restful expression of face at once captivated my affections and set up an emotional pulsation which, almost unconsciously, gave rise in my mind to the prophetic conception – This would be a nice wife for me. From that day onwards I was a frequent visitor and, after tea with the family, usually spent in her company a few most enjoyable hours, which on those occasions, invariably seemed exceedingly short.

In due course that mysterious sympathy which often arises between persons of the opposite sex when thrown much together, began to mutually develop in us and very soon we became greatly attached friends. At no time, however, during the four years of our acquaintance, did we ever arrange to meet outside the domestic circle. At length, as might have been expected, our social intercourse reached a happy climax and thus, on the 24th of May 1862 was reciprocally consummated, without doubt the greatest blessing of our future lives. . . On the fourth of September following we were united in wedlock at Meikle Geddes. From an early hour in the morning the rain had fallen in torrents and every one interested became greatly concerned as to what the state of the weather might be in the afternoon. By four o'clock, however, the sun was shining brightly in a cloudless sky and the sixty invited guests had all arrived. Half an hour later and my bride entered the room leaning on the arm of her uncle David. Neatly attired in a rich brown dress and bearing in her hand an elegant bouquet of green-house flowers, I, for a moment, doubted whether the handsome creature who was advancing to my side, was really the lady who had betrothed herself to me. She looked very sweet and pretty, and though at the time in her twenty-second year, the delicate rosy tint on her cheek, and the fresh clearness of her complexion, together with her petite size, made her appear as if she had been two or three years younger. As the minister was repeating the usual formula at the marriage ceremony, he inadvertently asked if I would promise to be 'a faithful and obedient wife', but instantly corrected the *lapus lingae* amid a suppressed titter among those present in the room. After numerous congratulations our friends sat down to an excellent dinner and thereafter adjourned to the granary for a most enjoyable dance in which some of the old men, who had not 'footed the light fantastic' for over thirty years, took part.

In September 1863, almost a year after our marriage, Mrs Thomson – who was in that condition incidental to married ladies – and myself went to Meikle Geddes where she was to remain until I returned from a short holiday with the Moir family near Aberdeen. Scarcely, however, had I arrived at Hilldowntree when a letter reached me stating that soon after my departure she had been visited by a little girl, who had come earlier than we expected. Nevertheless she was very welcome and I felt sure that her presence in the family would add, if possible, to our happiness and make the schoolhouse even more emphatically to us the 'spot of earth supremely blet'.

Next morning – Sunday – I received when in church, a telegram – 'Please come home with the first train, Mrs Thomson is ill'. This was a terrible shock and the anxiety which I endured all the long journey back was trying beyond anything I had ever experienced in the past. Entering her room toward sunset, I found that, owing to excessive wrappings and hot potations as the result of mistaken kindness on the part of her nurses, my wife was in a burning fever and well nigh raving for cold water, which they considered it extremely dangerous, in the circumstances, to allow her even to taste. After consultation in the evening with her medical attendant, Dr Grigor, a more rational treatment was inaugurated and strictly adhered to in the future. From that night forward she gradually regained strength, until by the time the holidays had come to an end she was able to take full charge of her lassie and attend to the duties of the household as formerly.

Extract from Robert Thomson's Cawdor notebook.
24 September 1865 – Remarkable providences: Being on a visit lately to a neighbouring town, myself and Mrs Thomson had occasion to meet with a poor but industrious old woman to whom we gave a shilling. On the road home, whilst talking of the propriety of what we had done, my eye was caught by a piece of bright silver which, proving to be a shilling, I picked up and thought that my liberality had been faithfully repaid.

Nor was the circumstance which occurred only a few days ago less worthy of note. A poor German, on his way home from America to Saxony, was wandering through this parish in search of work. Completely overcome with hunger and fatigue, he fell on the road perfectly exhausted and senseless. On his recovery I and a few friends collected a small sum and presented it to him before leaving. The Post brought me next morning a letter from an unexpected quarter containing just exactly twice the amount of my contributions.

Two years and four months had scarcely run their course when, on the thirtieth of December 1865, another member was added to our domestic circle. From careful inquiries I had found that the eldest son in my ancestral line had always borne the same Christian name, for at least six generations back and so, in accordance with this family tradition, we decided that our little boy should be called Robert.
Further extracts from Robert Thomson's Cawdor notebook.
30 Dec 1865 – This morning Mrs Thomson was safely delivered of a son. During the night there was a terrific storm of wind which caused much destruction of property both by sea and land.

2 January 1866 – Grandmama presented Baby with the sum of £30 from a deposit about which we were quite ignorant.

28 January – Robert was baptised today in the Cawdor Free Church by the Rev S.F. Maclauchlan.

30 January – Took dinner in the Cawdor Arms along with a company of upwards of 60 of the tenant farmers of Cawdor in honour of the marriage of the Earl's eldest daughter to Lieut.Col. Lambton of the 74 Scots Fusilier Guards.

8 March – Elected Secretary and Treasurer to the Nairnshire Farm Servants' Friendly Society.

13 March – Resigned the Secretarial office.

15 March – Much dissatisfaction prevails in the parish among the farmers who believe that the ultimate object of the Association is to agitate for an increase of wages. I am greatly blamed for helping the servants to accomplish their object from the circumstances of accepting office and revising the rules. I am much troubled on this account, seeing that the terms of the agreement were decidedly stated by me to a full meeting and were to the effect that I would immediately resign whenever any dissatisfaction bearing on the subject should be entertained.

18 March – My burden is relieved tonight. The Committee of the Nairnshire Farm Servants' Friendly Society met the Deacons' Court and, requesting the use of the Schoolroom, read the rules of the Society. Some of those who were loudest in declaiming the objects of the Association a few days ago have nothing to say, but all have given their opinion that it should be encouraged.

23 March – The Deacons' Court find that, owing to a clause in their lease, they have not the power to grant the Association the use of the School.

21 April – Minister does not take the proper view of the Government Inspector's Report of my school. It is as good as, in the circumstances, could have been expected. Two of the head teachers in the Presbytery have got worse reports this year, with twelve months to prepare, than I did with only two weeks.

29 May – This day last year Mama came to Cawdor. We have been mutually beneficial to each other but especially find her useful as a nurse. Mrs Thomson, to commemorate the event, gave us a very fine dinner.

6 June – The Free Church Education Committee, Edinburgh, found at the last term (Whitsunday) that they were in a position to pay the full yearly salary to the Teachers connected with their church, viz. £15. The Deacons' Court at Cawdor, although not bound to allow me the benefit of the additional £3.7s.6d, agreed at once to do so . . . Even this small sum will be of material service to our house, for which we desire the Father of gifts to enable us to cultivate grateful spirits, and thankfully acknowledge the liberal bounties of his gracious Providence.

30 June – Met with my brethren of the Nairnshire Teachers'

Association today in the parish schoolroom and afterwards dined at the Cawdor Arms. It was agreed that as different scales of fees existed in the County, an effort should be made to have an equalised minimum for all.

6 July – Mrs Thomson's aunt at Broomhill died on Wednesday morning last after an illness of about 4 years, during the greater part of which she suffered severely and was confined almost entirely to bed. A large number of friends and others attended the funeral today to the parish churchyard at Cawdor.

13 July – Tonight a dreadful thunderstorm passed over Cawdor, doing a good deal of damage to property in our neighbourhood. At Broomhill a valuable new horse was instantly struck down. At Newlands of Broomhill a few of the slates were thrown down, and a clock injured inside the house. A large oak tree at the castle was split and its bark detached round the whole stem. Few remember ever to have witnessed the lightning flash as continuously, or glare with such brilliancy. Our windows shook after each peal of thunder.

1 November – Gave the usual six weeks of autumn holidays on the 30th August. Spent a fornight of the vacation at Hilldowntree. Although much the better of our short stay, we were greatly disappointed to find that Mr D. Moir had been laid up for 12 weeks of paralysis in the legs, and during the time we were there he was seized with torpidity of the bowels. Neither the doctor nor his family apprehended any immediate danger, but he gradually sank after we left on Thursday morning and died on Saturday 29th of September at 7 am. We regretted much that we had come away so soon before. I did not go back for the funeral.

30 November – R. Thomson Jr. walked his first steps alone – 11 months old.

19 December – Went to Aberdeen on Saturday 8th to the Government Christmas Examination, which lasted from Monday 10th until Friday 14th embracing 10 subjects; about 30 candidates were present. Went out every night to Hilldowntree and felt greatly benefited both physically and intellectually.

1867

10 January – R. Thomson Jr. weaned.

25 March – Had a communication from the Lords of the Privy Council intimating that I had passed a successful examination at Marischal College [Aberdeen] in December 1866. May he who has bestowed on us this additional success, at the same time make us feel and acknowledge our obligations, and enable us as faithful stewards to use, so as not to abuse it.

6 April – Observed from their Lordships' Class List for December 1866, that I had passed 2nd Division, Third Degree.

17 May – Invested £100 in the Sutherland Railway Debentures for 3 years at 4½ per cent per annum – the due payment of the interest thereon being guaranteed by His Grace the Duke of Sutherland.

5 August – An unfortunate day – bled a boy's nose in School by mistake when at the same time a little girl fell senseless on the floor in a faint.

7 September – In company with Mr Macnaughton, Cawdor, I am to go and try the beneficial effects of the Strathpeffer mineral water for a week or two.

23 September 1867 – On coming to Strathpeffer we experienced little difficulty in procuring suitable lodgings . . . During the first few days we felt subject to a slight squeamishness, usually after taking some of the water. Most of our time was spent in climbing to the top of each of the surrounding eminences, including Ben Wyvis which was the feat of our stay. The view from the summit was not so extensive as we would have wished, nevertheless the extent of country laid before our vision was very great. A dense cloud passed over us while on the top which caused us some slight uneasiness, but it soon cleared off and we commenced our return – taking along with us some alpine club moss and a few specimens of very fine quartz. We drank ice cold water from a well within some few feet of the greatest height. The whole journey required eight hours. The distance was said to be 18 or 20 miles. In addition to the drinking hours, which were thrice a day when we drank a couple of tumblerfuls each time, we spent a good deal of our time in corresponding with our friends at home, and in giving a description of the Strath which appeared in the *Nairnshire Telegraph* of 18th as 'Notes from Strathpeffer'.

19 Oct – Opened the school on Monday last with 23 children. I feel rather anxious concerning the future as provisions are high and appearances indicate a lower attendance than usual.

30 Nov – Feel a good deal troubled because a few of my Scholars of the Free Church School, apparently without reason, are attending the parish school. 'Wherefore come these things upon me?' Jer. xiii.22.

7 December – Attended the annual meeting of the Nairnshire Teachers' Association, and was elected Secretary and Treasurer for 1868. Dined afterwards with the brethren in Anderson's Hotel, and spent a few hours pleasantly in social conversation.

1868

3 January – The usual winter holidays began on Christmas and ended with New Year's day. We had an invitation from the Moirs of

Hilldowntree to come and spend a few days there with our family, which however, Elsie thought impossible on account of the cold weather and the necessity of having someone at home during the repairs caused by dry rot on the floors and partitions of our sitting and side rooms. In these circumstances I was alone early on the road to the Nairn Station to get on with the first train which should have left about 7 o'clock am. That hour came and so did the train, but the ticket clerk was sound asleep in his bed and the key in his pocket. They said that he had partaken too freely of the inebriating cup the previous evening and the loudest screams of the steam whistle were wholly unavailing until more effective means were used to bring him to his post. This was done and in due course we arrived in Aberdeen . . .

22 Jan – An encouraging day. Received 20 shillings of Schoolpence, 10 pounds of very fine meat from a parent and a good many etceteras from Geddes . . .

24 Jan – A severe wind storm, accompanied with frost, snow and ultimately rain in the form of a cyclone, passed over Cawdor today. Only a few children were in school, and four of them ran a considerable risk in both coming to, and returning from school through the wood while hundreds of trees were falling. Our own house sustained only slight injuries – a few slates were blown down and part of the lead on the roof raised – being well sheltered by the adjoining wood on the south. At Meikle Geddes a part of the square was unroofed, corn and straw stacks overturned and the top of the hay stack thrown down in a few seconds by a powerful gust of wind. Most of the farm steadings around suffered more of less in like manner.

'At 10 am the velocity of the wind indicated by the anemometer was from 60 to 70 miles an hour. The heaviest gusts were about the hours of 11 and 12 am, and at these times the extraordinary velocity of 90 to 91 miles an hour was recorded – equivalent to a pressure on the square foot of 40.50 and 41.43 respectively. The whole horizontal movement of the air between 10 am of the 24th and 10 am of the 25th amounted to no less than 660 miles.' Arthur Fowler, Culloden.

31 Jan – Today there was a continuous and heavy downfall of rain, and by night the Nairn had risen far beyond the usual flood marks, causing no slight uneasiness to many who reside on the low grounds along its course. The force of the current has considerably shaken the Howford bridge and rendered the one on the south side of the town unsafe for even foot traffic. The drains about Viewhill are full to overflowing and the water is running in all direction – we are, however, quite safe.

13 February – Today Viscount Emlyn, eldest son of the Right Hon. the Earl of Cawdor, attained his majority, and about 140 of the tenantry and neighbouring county gentlemen received invitations to an excellent dinner given by his Lordship, in the guest hall of the

Castle. I received an invitation and was duly there at the hour appointed, 4.30 pm. For the occasion the hall was suitably fitted up, decorated and lighted with about 100 paraffin lamps and wax candles. A brass band from Inverness fitted the orchestra and played appropriate airs after each toast. Mr Stables, factor on the estate, occupied the chair and proposed the leading toasts of the evening. Major Rose, Kilravock, replied on behalf of the army in one of the most confused, rambling and broken speeches I have ever heard, and just when about to conclude, he asked the company to drink to the health of Lord Emlyn which, however, they had more sense than do. Most felt ashamed and everybody laughed. To the 'clergy of all denominations' the band played The Hundred psalm tune. After all was finished there was a grand pyrotechnic display of fireworks from the Castle tower.

Although the afternoon gave most unfavourable symptoms of mist and rain, it gradually wore off as the time approached for lighting the bonfires – a dozen of which blazed magnificently and shed thin lurid light far and wide. It is believed that one or more could be seen from Cairngorm to the coast of Caithness. At each there was a plentiful supply of 'real Brackla' [whisky], and the dancing and merriments which began around the towering flames were kept up with unflagging spirit till an early hour the following morning in the nearest convenient domicile.

18 February – Two children came to school today whose father had promised to send them eight months ago, but delayed from the affected want of shoes, clothes, or a desire to allow the vacation, new year or sacrament to be over – thus depriving them of a valuable part of their time available for education. It is a remarkable circumstance in my professional experience that a parent seldom keeps faith with the teacher in the matter of sending a child to school, according to a previous statement. The custom which principally obtains is to send on the day after the one on which they promised, frequently not until the following week, or, as in the above mentioned case, sometimes they fail to send them at all.

15 March – I.Scougal, HM Inspector, examined and inspected the school on Friday 13th inst. He was not in good humour when he came and in consequence, I believe that a few of the children failed in Arithmetic who would otherwise have performed their exercises quite correct.

18 April – The report which came on the 11th inst. stated the General Inspection as very satisfactory and the Individual Examination imperfect in the lower standards. In consequence the Lordships refused to issue my certificate until there was improvement in this respect. A full remittance of the year's claims was received today, and will materially increase our daily comforts, for which I trust we shall be made humbly thankful to our Heavenly Father.

1 October – One morning . . . I spent an hour or two in visiting Charleston of Nigg [near Aberdeen] where I spent 14 years of my youth before going to the Normal School at the age of 18. The general characteristics of the place are the same, but greatly improved with a few alterations. The race of inhabitants is entirely new with three exceptions, and I saw not a single one of my old associates – all have gone like myself, and most are engaged in the active pursuits of life. As I sauntered along looking at this object and at that, unknown faces gazed curiously at me through the windows and from the doors; the children, stopping from their amusements, scanned me from head to foot, and I strongly felt that I was a stranger.

I looked with peculiar interest at my old home – a small feu on which my mother erected two houses.

10 Oct 1868 – I began the last scholastic year with a good many doubts and fears regarding future prospects and success, but now at the end I am forced to acknowledge that God has disappointed all my evil forebodings and done for me much more than I had any conception of. The year just ended has been the best in a pecuniary point from school fees since coming to Cawdor. Similar feelings to those of last year occasionally pass over my mind now, but I hope, in reviewing the past, to receive grace and faith to enable me to go forward in the full assurance that 'My God for us will do all things well'.

12 Oct – Opened school today. There were 24 on the roll.

18 Oct – Showed a friend a few of Mrs Thomson's poetic compositions on which he pronounced very favourable opinion.

20 Oct – A few more of my scholars have this year again gone to the parish school, and being unable to discover a proper reason, I feel the matter very much . . .

24 Oct 1868 – This day ten years ago I left Aberdeen and came to Cawdor. The same morning my friend Mr David Moir Jr. entered Marischal College and had fair propects before him but, being seized with consumption, he died about two years afterwards . . . I came a young man of 20 years with comparatively little knowledge of men or things and with no worldly possessions beyond my clothing and a few books. Four years afterwards Miss Fraser of Meikle Geddes became my wife, and, by the blessing of God our union has in every repect been a most satisfactory and happy one. Our two children are very engaging and intelligent little creatures who, we trust, will be spared as a source of comfort to us and a credit to themselves . . . Since then my income has been increased about £20 per annum. On the whole, therefore, I have been as prosperous as could have been expected.

5 Dec – The Nairnshire Teachers' Association held their annual meeting in the Academy, Nairn. I was elected Vice President for the ensuing year and Mr Wedderspoon, Moyness read an able paper on

English Grammar. The members dined together and spent a couple of very agreeable hours in the Marine Hotel.

19 Dec – . . . One or two parents who, at the time I came to Cawdor, professed to be unalterably attached to the school and Free Church principles have suddenly turned hostile, withdrawn their children and sent them to the parish school. Other two families have, for apparently no sufficient reason, also done the same thing . . .

1869

9 Jan – Gave the Christmas holidays at the usual time, but to a fewer number than I ever had in school at this season . . .

18 March 1869 – The Deputation from the Nairn Free Presbytery . . . visited and examined the school today. In all branches the children made a very good appearance. One said there might be more elocution in the reading. They passed very well before H.M. Inspector on the same day the following week.

4 Sep 1869 – A few nights ago my friend Mr Macnaughton [parish schoolteacher] called on us as he frequently does, for the purpose of enjoying a few hours' congenial discussion on matters of both local and universal interest. Being near the time of our usual autumn vacation, we were talking over the way in which each might probably be inclined to occupy the whole or a part, when he told me that he had just been requested by the Right Hon. the Earl of Cawdor to come over to the Castle and give some lessons to one of his sons and two of his daughters. This he expected would necessitate his remaining at home for at least three or four weeks. Of course I congratulated him on being so fortunate, entertaining for him as I do the highest personal respect, but at the same time felt very downcast when I considered the small number of children that had attended the Free Church School during the previous year, and the relative professional respect it would secure for him in the eyes of many in the parish . . .

1870

19 Feb – The winter which has just come to a close has, in some respects, been more remarkable, both as regards its climatic changes and the consequent results to human health than many of its predecessors. Severe frost, occasionally relieved by dull fogs or a short rise of temperature above the freezing point, with a heavy fall of snow between Christmas and the New Year, made up a very cheerless season to everyone, but more especially to the poor and labouring

classes who, to a very large extent, depend for their support upon the clemency of the weather. Disease, tragedy and accident have each entered many a home-stead . . . The poisoned dart of the last enemy proved fatal to an aged member of our own family – Elsie's maternal uncle died at Meikle Geddes on the 24th December 1869 aged exactly 77 years and 9 months, and leaving no will the whole of his personal property and movable effects fall to be divided among two brothers, two sisters and the families of two sisters sometime deceased. The lease of the farm lapsed at Whitsunday 1868 and since that time he resided on the place as a tenant at will. The Earl of Cawdor now refuses to make a new agreement as he intends carrying into effect considerable changes beyond either the capacities or the desires of the resident mother and sister. Consequently they have been warned to remove at Whitsunday 1871 – an event which may be fraught with results, the ultimate effects of which may be more or less satisfactory to ourselves . . . Circumstances have, in many cases for sometime back, been unfavourable to us . . . The number of children attending the school has very greatly decreased and our income from fees has correspondingly been reduced. Lastly, though of small moment, in renewing a debenture loan for £100 with the Sutherland Railway Company I had to take 10% per annum less interest than formerly, owing to the cheap rate of money in the market . . .

5 Aug – Lord and Lady Emlyn invited the children attending the Parish and Free Church Schools to come to the Castle tonight and partake of tea on the lawn in honour of the christening of their infant son and heir, Hugh Archibald Vaughan Campbell . . . Everyone was pleased and the fête will be long remembered by the rising generation of Cawdor.

6 September – Today Mr Macnaughton and I went to a place called Craig-a-Clach about 6 miles up the burn of Cawdor where a very brittle kind of Cairngorm stone is to be found, but of no value. We brought home some average specimens. From the top of the hill immediately above the Craig a most beautiful and extensive landscape presents itself to the view, combining in pleasant variety, the scenery of mountain land and cultivated plain with a wide expanse of ocean stretching between for many miles from east to west.

15 Sept – Today my mother passed away into the world of spirits . . . Thus at the age of 73 she has passed away full of days and, we hope, ripe for an eternal residence in the Kingdom of Glory. Upwards of five years ago she came from Aberdeen to live with us in Cawdor on account of advancing years and failing ability to manage her domestic concerns. We both have endeavoured to perform our filial duty in a manner becoming our obligations and responsibility; nor have we been left without the satisfaction of knowing that she fully appreciated our exertions in this respect. During her stay here, our

intercourse has been of the most felicitous nature which renders the blank in our view the more conspicuous, and the loss of her prudent and wise counsels very much missed, as circumstances arise from time to time which require considerations and caution. Notwithstanding a natural shortness of vision she had committed large portions of the Scriptures and most of the Psalms to memory, and read over and over again Dr Meikle's works, Harvey's *Meditations* etc and Dr Young's *Night Thoughts*, to each of which she became deeply attached, and delighted much to ponder upon their instructive contents when engaged in any operation not requiring direct mental attention. Her manner and customs were simple and unaffected, but sincerely respectful to everyone; in each transaction she was particularly considerate and studied to execute it with startling honesty; endeavouring in all cases to be scrupulously faithful in every engagement and as a rule performed beyond her promise. In Biblical knowledge she was very intelligent, taking a lively interest in ecclesiastical matters and enjoyed through life a gratifying intercourse with many friends much higher than herself in the social scale. By respectful industry and economy she managed to live in easy circumstances, at the same time procuring a good education for myself, and also to save a very considerable portion of a small sum of money left by my father at his death. She had a great desire to see her family comfortably settled in life, and this was granted in the fullest extent. I had taught with fair success for upwards of 14 years, been united to a most amiable and dutiful partner, had saved and inherited a pretty large sum of money, with a certain prospect, if spared in ordinary circumstances, of getting considerable additions, which under the Divine blessing would secure to us a competent portion of worldly good. And just when failing nature had begun to render the comforts of life no longer enjoyable, she was called away to the higher existence of spiritual life.

1871

25 March – This morning our little Robert, while lifting a drink of water from a somewhat dangerous well near us, slipped his foot and fell in up to the middle in the water. In a very providential manner he succeeded in getting out himself, no help being at the time near, and thus escaped death by drowning in a very wonderful way. In the evening Mrs Maclauchlan died at the Free Church manse, after a ten days' illness, and left her husband, the minister, a lonely old man and without any near relation to take care of him in the midst of declining years and accompanying infirmities.

29 April – We have just contributed our last mark of outward

respect for the mortal remains of Grandma, by erecting over her grave a head tombstone . . .

1872

13 July – Today we got the minister's conveyance and, locking the door, drove out with whole family first to Broomhill and then to the Bog that Grandma [Mrs Thomson's mother] might see her friends once more in their own homes, where she had not been for six years previous, and be refreshed with a drive in the open air. Day fine. We were all much pleased. The children were delighted . . .

18 October – Stayed at home during the holidays this season as excursion pleasure is much marred on account of Elsie requiring to stay with the old people. This to both of us, is duty and not much of a sacrifice, for when I look around upon some of my nearest neighbours and see the troubles they have to bear – often the result of carelessness or simplicity – then make a comparison with my own happy home and family, I feel that surely, though we want not trials even in our own lots, we have been made an exception to the general order of things.

One family near us work unitedly for more than my own income, yet possess little comfort, no luxury and are always from hand to mouth. Three or four times a year they get drunk at once for a couple of days or so, eat nothing during that time, then for several days thereafter suffer from the effects of a deranged system . . . James Clunas Esq., Nairn, has sent his son William to stay here for a few weeks, and he and Ettie and Robert have been revising lessons for about two hours daily. This has profitably engaged part of our time.

The people of Scotland and especially the rural classes, being deeply impressed with the value of a sound intellectual training for their sons and daughters, had for many years, been pressing the Government to introduce a national system of elementary education by which the poorest boy might be able to pursue his studies from the parish school right on to the University. At last, after numerous failures, Lord Advocate Young succeeded in passing a comprehensive measure and in March 1873 my scholars were examined for the last time under the old regulations by one of Her Majesty's denominational inspectors. A few days afterwards the local Free Church Presbytery too, closed its connection with my school. Although on these occasions the various religious and secular tests were pretty stiff, yet the children did very well and were highly complimented by the individual members for the appearance they had made. Henceforward the School Board becomes the controlling power and the annual inspections, on behalf of the Education Department, will be conducted without reference to the teacher's personal creed . . .

Having as usual, laid aside the reins of office for a few weeks in autumn (1873), we decided one day to pay a short visit to the Nairn poor-house. Only recently erected it is a plain but substantial building containing accommodation for seventy five inmates, though there were only twenty men, women and children present when we looked in. Paupers, owing to the necessary restrictions exercised over their freedom, entertain strong prejudices against the reputed treatment of those who have been sent here but when it is remembered that the indigent, who apply for relief have, as a rule, failed in life, one cannot help thinking that they ought to be very grateful, that, by the laws of our country ever essential provision, as I thought, had been made for them during the remainder of their lives. Outside, the grounds are ample and to those who are able to work there is easy employment found for them either in the kitchen garden, or among the flower beds, while the apartments within are all kept spotlessly clean, warm and well lighted . . .

Next year, in reply to the usual invitation to spend a few weeks with the Moir family at Hilldowntree, we stated that we had decided for several reasons to stay at home. By a later post however, we received a letter from Mr Moir informing us that, as he had just been appointed manager of the Fair Field Iron Works in Colombo, Ceylon, and requiring to start as early as possible, we would need to reconsider the matter and come on. Accordingly we did so and on arrival found his mother wonderfully cheerful and resigned. A day or two after we paid a visit to the light-house at Girdleness. Serving as a landmark by day, it shows a powerful light to guide mariners in the darkness of night to avoid a very rocky coast. The ascent is made by an inside spiral stair of one hundred and seventy eight steps. On reaching the lantern at the top, we carefully inspected the great lamp with its beautiful diopteric lenses and relative prisms. On our return journey we passed the new breakwater in course of erection at the entrance to the Aberdeen harbour. Here the children were much pleased in watching the operations – especially the divers in their peculiar dresses as they descended to, or rose from their work, at a depth of some thirty [feet] below the surface of the water. Here they were laying the foundation of a great wall with large blocks of concrete weighing, we were told, in most cases over twelve tons.

On the following Saturday, as Mrs Moir goes to reside in Aberdeen, the final parting came at Hilldowntree where, for twenty years we had enjoyed the closest friendship, and felt as much at home as round our own fireside . . .

CHAPTER 4

Across to Ardclach

Since the passing of the Scotch Education Act of 1872, we have been handed over by the Free Church Deacon's Court to the Cawdor School Board who resolved, at a recent meeting, to provide for our children by enlarging the present parochial building at the village. In these circumstances, Elsie and I thought it expedient to be on the outlook for another situation. When therefore, we learned that a teacher was wanted for the neighbouring Public (late Parish) School of Ardclach, I decided – Mr Stables being chairman of both Boards – to make formal application. A few weeks afterwards I received a private letter from Mr James McPherson, Farmer, Clunas, stating that 'To all appearance at our meeting today, there is every chance of your succeeding.' In due course, Mr Riach the Clerk, wrote announcing that I had been appointed from a list of seventeen candidates at a salary of £100 plus the Schoolhouse and garden, with the probability of being chosen Registrar for the Parish.

During the few ensuing weeks we were busily engaged in preparing for our early removal. Altogether forty to fifty of the parents and parishioners called at the schoolhouse to bid us a kindly farewell, while the farmers in the neighbourhood offered to give us every help with men and horses. Accordingly on the 30th December 1873, Robert's birthday, our furniture and fuel, of which we had a considerable quantity, were carefully packed on eleven carts and reached our new home with the breakage of only one tea cup! Next Monday, the 5th of January, we opened school at Ardclach with a fair attendance of scholars.

Ardclach School Log Book records 18 boys and 15 girls in April.

On Sunday the 5th of July I was ordained an Elder, along with Peter Grant, Carnoch; George Fraser, Tachter; and Alexander Mackintosh, Ballville, in the Free Church of Ardclach. After my election I resolved not to accept office and wrote to the moderator of the session to that effect, but in deference to the representations of Mr John Mackillican, Achagour and the minister who told me that my name was on every voting paper, I ultimately agreed and, at the conclusion of the special service, signed the Formula.

(26th August) Today we all paid a visit to the Channel Fleet now lying off Invergordon in the Cromarty Firth. The day could scarcely have been finer and our sail was most enjoyable. On arriving, the captain put us on board the 'Devastation' and 'Ajincourt' two of the finest vessels in the British navy and left us for two hours on each. We entered into pleasant conversation with many of the mariners who conducted us over their respective ships and appeared specially pleased to tell us all about the 'Woolwich Infants', which are capable of doing such fearful damage at great distances. On our return voyage we touched at Cromarty, a decayed old fashioned seaport. We went to see the house where Hugh Miller was born, and examined very carefully his collection of Old Red Sandstone fossils, especially *Pterichthys Milleri* and *Coccosteus decipiens* etc., duplicates of which are in the British Museum. Nearby, a monument with full length statue atop has been erected on an eminence beside the churchyard where, while working as a letter-cutter on the tombstones, Hugh met the young lady, Lydia, who afterwards became his wife.

Ardclach School Log Book: 13 November 1874 – The School Board provided 23 slates for the use of the infants under the Mistress – each one, if broken, to be replaced or the price charged to the child doing so . . . (H.M. Inspector's Report 5 June 1875 – 'Some effort should be made to correct the present extremely irregular attendance, as it prevents the teacher from doing himself justice . . .'. 26 November 1875 – One child died who was in school the previous week – her brother died on 10 December (Margery and Duncan Mackintosh of E. Belivat). February 1877 – Child no 21 on roll left for Village School [Ferness] on receiving a letter of warning for irregular attendances.

Mrs Fraser, my mother-in-law, late of Meikle Geddes, died with us at Ardclach on the 4th of April 1878 at 1.35pm. For the previous two weeks she had been confined to bed from an attack of atonic dyspepsia, accompanied with great difficulty in breathing, but when an angry sore broke out a few days later on the right leg, and continued to freely discharge serum, her strength gradually decreased thereafter till the end came. After due consideration Mrs Thomson and I decided to be the first in the parish to give no

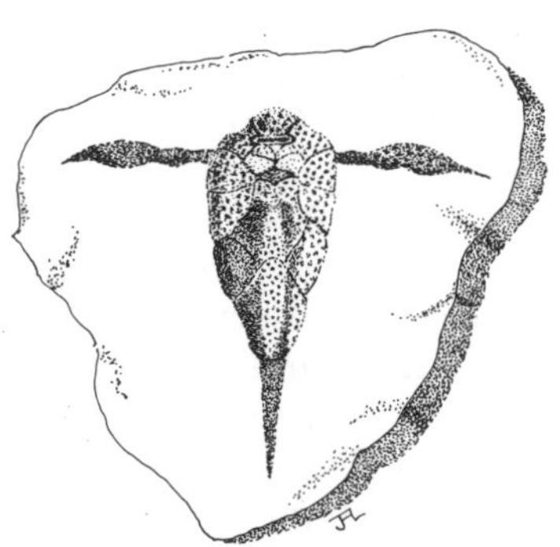

The fossil fish Pterich-thys Millen

spirits at the funeral, and to 'lift' the body promptly at the hour appointed. This was done in the hope that our example might be thenceforward followed, in discontinuing a very needless and much abused custom on such solemn occasions. Accordingly, though we failed to enlist the sympathy of our minister Mr Macdonald, the interment took place on the next Saturday, without 'refreshments' in the grave yard of Geddes under the table-stone beside the remains of her late brothers David and John MacFarquhar, or MacDonald.

Ardclach School Log Book: 5 July 1878 Inspector's Report – The attendance at this school appears to be very irregular . . . [which] must be taken into account in estimating the character of the instruction, on which it would act injuriously. The results in the lower standards are good on the whole, and would, I have no doubt, have been better had the books been more suitable. Grammar in the fourth and fifth standards is much behind and Dictation and Arithmetic are only pretty good. More accuracy must be shown in Geography and History next year, otherwise the Grant will not be recommended. The children presented in special subjects passed well. Singing good. Sewing and knitting fair . . .

One afternoon, in the following autumn, the Rev Mr Mackenzie, parish minister, asked me over to the Manse to meet his friends, Colonel and Mrs Grant of Nile celebrity. Both were exceedingly courteous and, as a matter of course, the subject of conversation between the Colonel and myself was almost entirely confined to his many notable experiences in India or Africa. After the mutiny of his native Bengal regiment in 1857 he was attached to the 78th Highlanders and distinguished himself at the relief of Lucknow, where he was severely wounded. In 1860, along with his great friend Captain Speke, he explored the Victoria Nyanza and followed the Nile far enough down to establish its identity with the great river of Egypt. He had a remarkably fine physique, standing six feet two inches and otherwise developed in proportion. He was, I soon found, an excellent Botanist and an ardent lover of Nature. In his 'walk across the Dark Continent' he gathered a valuable collection of native plants, not a few of which were found to be new to science. These, in all probability, will, in due course, be handed over to the national Herbarium at Kew.

After the usual official visit of Her Majesty's Inspector to our school in June 1879 my Certificate was called for revision to the Education Department, when their Lordships, in consideration of the various records endorsed thereon, returned it raised to the First Class. This was very gratifying to both Mrs Thomson and myself as, henceforward, no further entries will require to be made. Twelve months later Elsie and Robert went to Aberdeen for the Local University examinations and each passed very creditably in the whole course. Robert in addition, took papers for the Ordinary

Certificate and came out with distinction in Arithmetic, History, Geography, Bible Knowledge and Physiography. In recognition that he had obtained the highest place in the last subject, he received a complimentary prize, 'Evenings at the Microscope' by P.H. Gosse.

Next year we sent [young Robert] to Dingwall to sit as a candidate for one of the bursaries offered by the Society for Propagating Christian Knowledge in Scotland and, heading a list of twelve, he was awarded one of £18 for a year to enable him to prosecute the higher studies at Rainings School under Dr MacBean, in Inverness. After finishing his term here, he was examined in the Free Church Manse of Ardclach and gained a McPhail bursary with the view of possibly deciding for the ministry but, not being able to speak Gaelic, could not hold it. In the following November he went to the Edinburgh University and matriculated in Arts. Next year he passed the medical preliminary examination and ultimately became in 1889 a graduate, M.B;C.M. of Aberdeen.

School Log Book: 13 December 1878 – Ten inches of snow, quarter of roll in attendance. 24 December – Over two feet in depth. Christmas holidays were not to be given this year but the school had to be closed to 2nd January, even then no children could come in the first week.

6 February 1880 – Roll 56. Children include those from Dunearn, Collindown, Bobbin Mill, Drummore, Logie Bridge, Achagour, Banchor, Ferness, Manse, March Stripe, Wester Dulsie and 'Hollybush', Ardclach, Moss-side.

26 November 1880 – storm continues and no children during week. Twenty inches of snow. 3 December – still no children, measles. 24 December – no holidays were to be given but no children could come anyway.

January 1881 – weather still inhibiting.

27 June 1881 – school deficient in inkwells, a clock and suitable maps. Two small forms needed, and a new lock on the schoolroom door.

CHAPTER 5

Jottings from our Journal, by Elsie Fraser Thomson, the Schoolhouse

1882

January (4th) In connection with the New Year festivities, my husband and I, along with a few neighbours, dined in the evening at the Established Manse, where the hospitable Genius is seldom absent. With the rare faculty of making every thing move sweetly in our social intercourse, Mr and especially Mrs Mackenzie, without apparent effort, have the distinctive charm of imparting a high moral tone to the general conversation at any domestic function with which they may care to associate themselves. Gentle and unassuming, they both live a life of genuine integrity, kindness and active benevolence, whenever it may be needed in the parish. The dinner table was lovely and no pains were spared to make each one feel comfortable and truly happy. (31st) Busy arranging classes and attending to several other relative duties in school but despite the little troubles which, at times, crop up and have to be overcome, I very much like the children and my work. In the afternoon Robert and I went over to Achagour and were very pleased to find Mrs Mackillican much better than we had expected, considering the rather serious illness through which she has just passed.

February (10th) An old pupil, Mr Tocher from Cawdor having received a situation in one of Mr James Mackillican's tea gardens in Darjeeling we joined the dinner party that was invited to Achagour in order to bid him farewell before sailing to enter upon his new sphere of labour in the far East. This appointment is very encouraging and, let us hope, that the young man may not only prove a faithful servant to his respected master but in time become a worthy example to other lads in his parish and even an honour to the country he is soon to leave behind.

Ardclach School Log: Floor found by the Inspectors to be very dirty and washed only twice a year. 'The offices' too are very dirty and the children are standing on the seat!

May (9th) Elsie had a very enjoyable drive to Lochindorbh with Mr and Mrs Macdonald of the Free Church Manse here. After the minister had discharged his professional duties among a few families belonging to his flock in the district, he and the two ladies paid a visit by boat to the ruins of the Wolfe of Badenoch's famous stronghold on the island near the north end. In moving about among the old walls they discovered a Jackdaw's nest in a deep crevice beside the principal gateway. The eggs, five in number, must have been a third, or even a fourth laying, as they were of a very pale green colour with only one or two of the usual darker markings on the shells at the larger end. Two are now in our cabinet and much prized as a great ornithological curiosity. (26th) Our school was examined to-day by Mr Jolly, H. M. Inspector, and after he remained to look over the Natural History collection of local plants and insects in my husband's cabinet. He was greatly pleased with what Robert had already accomplished and suggested that we should make frequent use of the various specimens, in order to encourage the children to search for, and take a practical interest in, the common objects of the woods and waysides.

Ardclach School roll twenty two boys and twenty four girls.

July (1st) Our son, Robert, having prepared two essays in connection with the Free Church Welfare of Youth scheme, we are very pleased to find that he has been awarded a couple of Certificates – one for 'Moses' and the other for 'The Shorter Catechism'.

Ardclach School Log Book: Inspector's Report – This school continues to be taught with great vigour and devotedness, and very good order. Pupils very tidy, but still shy and wanting in vigour . . . Walls should be washed . . . Proper arrangements must be made for cleaning out the 'offices' regularly.

(7th) Our kind friend and neighbour, the Rev. Colin Mackenzie, the Manse of Ardclach, died this afternoon at half past one o'clock. He was much respected as a gentleman, and especially so for his liberal views and kindly disposition towards everyone, without distinction, throughout the parish. He did much to tone down that unchristian spirit of religious bitterness towards the Establishment, kindled and fanned by the ministers of the Free Church, among their people, after the Disruption. I had the sorrowful pleasure of helping to arrange a great number of wreaths at the manse, before the remains were taken downstairs. There was a large funeral and many female friends assembled in a body on the rock beside the grave yard to witness the interment of a man who never tired in seeking to faithfully discharge his duty. On all hands, it was admitted that it will be long before Ardclach will look upon another minister like honest Colin Mackenzie. On the following Sunday a good many even of the Free Church body went 'down the brae', from both sides of the river, to hear his funeral sermon from the text – 'There remaineth, therefore a rest for the people of God'. Next day we went along and placed a beautiful wreath of Forget-me-nots on the grave.

(29th) Received note from Achagour asking Robert and myself to go over for the night, as Mr Mackillican was very low. On our arrival, we found him conscious but unable to speak. He looked earnestly at Robert as if he wished him to take worship. Having done so, he cordially shook him by the hand and closed his eyes for the last time. While we all sat beside him, he passed peacefully away at five o'clock the next morning and I remained to dress the body . . .

For upwards of half a century John Mackillican was tenant of Achagour and greatly esteemed as one who at all times took a deep interest in any movement which was calculated to be for the good of the parish. In church matters he sympathized, at an early period, with the Evangelical section and, at the Disruption in 1843, he unhesitatingly cast in his lot with the Free Church and ever since has been a much respected elder in her communion. The generous hospitality dispensed at Achagour was well known and at no time was he more delighted than when one or more ministers along with a band of worthy associates, sat at his table in connection with the spiritual interests of the local congregation.

October (1st) Spent a few days at Torrich and went to the Free Church with the Macpherson family on Sunday. It quite gladdened our hearts to meet so many kind cheery friends who had evidently not forgotten us. On our return Mrs Mackenzie and her sister of the Ardclach Manse, in preparing to leave their beautiful home for a house in Nairn, sent me a large number of useful and ornamental articles as parting gifts, which we all appreciate very much as substantial tokens of a long and very sincere friendship.

In the morning, after packing my son's box for his first session at the Aberdeen University, we had a good view of the great comet now passing our earth. For several weeks it has been a most brilliant object in the heavens and seems to be following in the same track as those of 1843 and 1880. The tenuity of the tail is inconceivable to us as the stars, which the slightest fog would conceal, are seen to shine clearly through the countless thousand miles of its impalpable material. It is certain, we are told, that on not a few occasions our earth must have come within the vapour of a comet's tail but with what decided influence, no one seems able to say. It is a popular idea however, that fruit is all the better, as we find the vintages of the years referred to being advertised as specially fine comet wines. Astronomers tell us that its orbit is so far extended into space that it will take seven hundred years before it can complete the circuit and return to human view.

November (12th) On our way to church I had a note by a messenger to go over to Achagour. Arrived just in time to close the eyes and see the end of our dear friend Mrs Mackillican. Had the sorrowful pleasure of 'taking about' and dressing the body of one who was greatly respected for many years over a wide district. In the evening not a few of the neighbours called at the house to sympathize with the family and remained to hold a religious service in the evening before leaving. (15th) At Achagour all day in connection with the funeral. Fourteen sat down to dinner after their return from the church yard. Again Elsie gave refreshments to a number of old Cawdor friends in the Schoolhouse. (29th) The Established Church Congregation have elected the Rev. David Miller, Brechin, to be the minister of Ardclach.

December (6th) About two o'clock in the afternoon my husband erected his telescope in the garden and we had an excellent view of the Transit of Venus. The planet appeared like a very considerable dark spot, slowly gliding across the sun's face, as on a sea of pearly white. Owing to its rather dense atmosphere there was a narrow ring of brilliant silvery light surrounding its tiny disc. As this beautiful phenomenon will not occur again until June 2004 we have witnessed today what no human being now on earth can ever hope to look upon during life here. This is the planet whose movements in the sky appeared so erratic to the astronomer King Alphonso the tenth of Castile, that he said, 'Had I been present at the Creation, I could have given some good advice'!

(15th) The weather for some days past, has been extremely cold, and the falling snow, driven with the utmost impetuosity in clouds of blinding drift, has accumulated with alarming rapidity in every possible situation.

Ardclach School Log Book: Low attendance at school.

This morning, on raising the blind of our bedroom window we were delighted to observe a pair of famished Partridges feeding very affectionately in a sunny corner near the door, on a patch of soft grass. Taking alarm at some slight noise in the kitchen, they took to flight but returned about midday on foot, bringing with them a covey of six other associates, probably equally necessitous. After breakfast I entertained a flock of poor hungry Chaffinches, Hedge-sparrows, Yellow-hammers, along with a Mavis, a Robin and a Blackbird to a comfortable meal on the footpath. In the afternoon a few Rooks, having heard apparently of my thoughtful generosity, presented themselves with ruffled plumage in the apple tree and, looking anxiously for a share of my hospitality, were not turned away empty.

(30th) My dear son's birthday. May he grow in Grace as he advances in years.

1883

Ardclach School Log Book: 5 January – School at Knockandhu opened on 2nd inst. under Miss Caroline Murdoch, Lynemore.

February (10th) Today we had the unusual experience of receiving a bridal party, along with the officiating clergyman and witnesses, at the Schoolhouse in order to fill up and sign the necessary Marriage Schedule, which the bridegroom, in his joy, had neglected to call for previous to the nuptial ceremony at Little Mill the day before.

March

Ardclach School Log Book: Snow storms closed the school most of the month.

(16th) The snow storm, which has become alarmingly severe, still continues and my bird pensioners are all constant in their attendance whenever I appear outside. A poor Rook sits anxiously in the apple tree nearby and gratefully partakes of any scraps I care to give him. On Sunday the roads were almost impassable and, in consequence, only three persons were present at Divine service in the Established and two in the Free.

April (3rd) We received a letter from Mrs Lightbody, Jersey City, New York, containing an order for £3 on behalf of a poor old man living at Burnside, Auldearn. Her late husband who was a native of Ardclach, had formerly taken an interest in him when in America and, now that he had returned and was in reduced circumstances, she wished to let him know that he had not been forgotten. After schoolhours we visited several sick people in the parish and found every one exceedingly kind and glad to see us. Pleased to observe my son's name in the 'Inverness Courier' as being specially recommended for Greek Literature in his University. (19th) Mr Macleod, H.M.Inspector examined the school today, and we both feel so happy that every one presented in the six standards got a full pass – a clean sheet, indeed. Rachel Sinton, one of my pupils, brought me a beautiful bouquet of flowers to ornament the dinner table, and Mrs Brodie of Lethen sent a letter expressing her sorrow at not being able to be present. The following week Mr Macleod paid a 'visit without notice' but found everything in complete order and, after the required entry in the Log Book, he and his lady remained to tea. (28th) This is my birthday. In the evening Mr Moir of Ceylon presented Elsie with a very artistic solid silver necklet and a pair of bracelets all made to his order from Indian rupees and she is very proud of them. Uncle has not been keeping well.

June (17th) A lad from Lochindorbh – eight miles distant – came this morning as a scholar and states that he will think nothing of walking up and down for a few months in order to improve his education. (29th) A present of trout came from Lochindorbh today and in the afternoon Robert, along with two fellow students, William Gordon and Charles Mann, arrived here from Aberdeen, having made the journey over the hills on foot in three days by way of Deeside, Cairngorm and Grantown on Spey.

August (8th) A lot of presents from parents and a large parcel of trout from Lochindorbh for the third time. This is very kind and we ought to be exceedingly grateful to a munificent Providence.

September (4th) This is the anniversary of our marriage and I am thankful to acknowledge that our union has been an exceedingly happy one. After breakfast we drove to Whitemire, near Darnaway, on our usual autumn visit. The day was fine and the sun shone out bright and warm from a cloudless sky. All the way down we enjoyed the beauty of the lovely autumn flowers which grew in great profusion along the wayside. Mr and Mrs Rose did everything they could to make our social intercourse as pleasant and happy as possible. After dinner we all took a walk over to Darnaway Castle. Mrs Ronald received us very kindly and showed us much that was interesting in the various rooms. Randolph's Hall is a magnificent apartment where, it is said, the Earl could assemble a thousand men-at-arms before setting out on some feudal expedition among the neighbouring clans. Here too, has been witnessed many a brilliant social spectacle when the ladies shone in all the richest and gayest varieties of silks, while anon the whole area would become a scene of imposing grandeur, that in the merry dance, was perpetually moving, mixing and changing. By the time we were ready to leave Whitemire, the sky had become overcast and rain fell most of the way but, being fully prepared, we got home very comfortably.

(15th) Took a [trip] along with Mr James Moir of Ceylon to Lochindorbh. To save time we partook of luncheon on the journey, but when we arrived at Terriemore we had to join the Macdonald family and sit down at their hospitable board. Having finished, their son John, brother of our pupil, got the boat in readiness and placed his service at our disposal for the afternoon. After rowing us all round the loch he landed us on the island in order that we might look over

Darnaway Castle

the ruins of the fine old stronghold, the famous mountain seat of the Wolfe of Badenoch . . .

October

Ardclach School Log Book: Received from Inverness and Ross and Nairn Club four medals for 3rd, 4th, 5th, and Higher classes.

(31st) A beautiful grey granite obelisk has just been erected in the Church Yard to the memory of our respected friend, the late Rev. Colin Mackenzie, and the tradesmen are busy fitting up a chaste marble tablet inside the church near the pulpit. Sent some refreshment to those who were engaged in the work.

November (26th) This morning and forenoon I was so much taken up with callers, and afterwards with a band of tinkers, that I had no time for any breakfast! My intercourse however, with the former was so pleasant that I did not much miss it.

December (7th) Mr Henry, Watchmaker, Nairn, set up in the Free Church, the clock which was gifted to the congregation in his Will by the late Mr John Mackillican. In the evening we went over to Achagour to dinner and before leaving Mr Pryse [Mackillican] gave me a present of specially fine tea. On my return I found that Mrs Mackenzie, late of the Manse, had sent me a very nice Christmas cake.

1884

January (1st) As a new year's present, Uncle gave Elsie a small nugget of Australian gold, which was sent home some years ago by his brother William, and we find that there is quite enough to make a thick ring. (24th) This is a very stormy day. The snow is deep and our windows are almost closed with drift, but I received a large piece of beef and several white puddings from Lynemore and am grateful to record that we have every comfort inside. A flock of small birds and a few Rooks came to the door begging for crumbs so they were not disappointed.

February

Ardclach School Log Book: 1 February – 'phenomenal cyclone' blocked the roads with snow. Barometer 27.466 at Nairn. Almost no children through the week.

(13th) In connection with the forthcoming ploughing match at Fleenas my husband wrote out a long speech for the chairman who desires to eulogize a well known gentleman who had given the Association a few valuable prizes. Heard on our way to church that a neighbour, poor Donald Macqueen, died in the evening before, in his chair when in the act of closing his bible after having read the usual chapter at family worship.

April (16th) A couple of tourist gentlemen, Edward and Henry Wilson, each an M.A. of Cambridge from Forncett Rectory, Norfolk, were 'doing' the Findhorn and having failed to get a bed at either of the manses called at the schoolhouse, so at some inconvenience I took them in for the night. Finding that they were greatly interested in Natural History, Robert showed them his collection of plants, eggs and insects. They were not a little surprised and we thereafter had a very enjoyable scientific conversation till late in the evening. (21st) Had a letter from our visitors stating that they had accomplished their purpose and that they were to stay for some weeks with Sir J.P. Grant of Rothiemurchus before returning to England. (26th) Gave some refreshment to three men who were searching the river for the body of a herd-boy who is believed to have been drowned while trying to cross the stream on his way home.

May (6th) Within the last few days I have been made the recipient of a great number of presents from the children's parents – rabbits, warm milk, butter, eggs, and a bag of potatoes. (21st) The remains of the poor [lad] who had gone astray were found, greatly decomposed in a pool on the Findhorn, near Sluie. (23rd) Our school was examined and the Inspector appeared to be very well pleased with the result. He remained to lunch and seemed in good spirits.

June (6th) H.M. Inspector paid a 'surprise' visit. Everything was found in proper order and he and Mrs Macleod remained to tea. (19th) Went out with Robert for an entomological walk in the Dulsie Wood where I found a beautiful specimen of the Miller Moth *Acronycta leporina*, which is always considered a rarity and, as yet, it is the only sample of the family in our cabinet.

August (9th) The Secretary of the Nairn Arts Exhibition Committee, having asked the favour of showing our Natural History collection in the Public Hall, my two Roberts took down and arranged on the stall, all the plants, insects and eggs without the least mishap and many visitors from the south seemed to be greatly interested in our upland specimens. (12th) Our two good neighbours, Messrs Simpson and Sinton, were here to-night and 'drummed' a swarm of bees into an empty hive. When finished they handed me about seventy pounds of excellent honey. In performing this curious operation our friends got frequently stung but, from past experience being so thoroughly innoculated with the virus, it had ceased to produce in them any of the usual uncomfortable effects.

October (4th) This morning, our bedroom window being slightly open at the bottom a tiny Wren and a Robin-redbreast came in for a few minutes to salute us before rising and no doubt, according to the Legend, warn us that in a short time we would hear some important news, either favourable or otherwise. In the evening we had an unclouded view of a total eclipse of the moon. This beautiful phenomenon, different from a solar one, is visible on all parts of the earth's surface opposite the sun. Before the dawn of astronomical science, superstition gave various reasons for the occurrence and not a few stories are told of the learned turning their correct knowledge to account; for example, Columbus, when in a great strait for provisions, procured them in abundance from the natives of Jamaica through the prediction of a lunar eclipse which would, he assured them, put out the light of their moon. (16th) Within the past few days I have received much kindness – a chicken, eggs, butter and milk, sent with the school children, while my husband got £3 from Mr T.D. Brodie, Esq. of [Coulmony] for prizes. (17th) Our pretty black cat, 'Arabi' came home today after having been away in the woods for over a month. Several times before, he has been off for a fortnight but I am afraid, though he is favoured by the game-keepers, if he repeats this often, he will come to grief some day.

(19th) Heard with a deep sorrow that our dear friend Mrs Mackenzie, late of the Manse, passed away this morning at ten o'clock in Nairn. We are to send a wreath of flowers from our garden for her coffin. (22nd) This afternoon the remains were consigned to rest in the 'Narrow House', beside the minister, in the Ardclach Church-yard. Robert attended the funeral a great part of the way and I, with many a sincere sympathizer, viewed the last service from the adjoining rock on the river side. Possessed of uncommon personal attractions, refined manners together with charming conversational powers Mrs Mackenzie presided, with great dignity, for thirty years over the unbounded hospitalities of the Manse table and delighted all who had the priviledge of enjoying her society. On the Sabbath following, the Rev. Mr Miller at the close of his sermon, feelingly referred to the sad event and when he wound up his remarks with the text slightly altered – 'Lovely and pleasant were they in their lives, and by death they were not long divided', the preacher was visibly affected and many in the congregation were moved to tears . . .

1885

January . . . (12th) My son has been appointed Surgeon to the steam ship 'Resolute' of Dundee, Captain Jackman, and will sail on the 17th for the Newfoundland seal fishing. Thereafter she will proceed to search for whales in the far north. There are sixty five of a crew, nine large boats and a steam launch. As the ship appears to have been well provisioned, we hope all on board will be very comfortable during her long voyage.

February (25th) Had a letter from Robert in which he states that after a rather slow and stormy passage the 'Resolute' arrived at St John's without the least mishap. The scenes and customs in the New World impressed him as being different in many respects from those in our country.

March (2nd) Elsie has been asked to sing at a local concert on behalf of a poor girl who lost an arm by the steam thrashing mill at Dulsie. Had a letter from Mr Moir bidding us good-bye, as he is just about to leave for Bombay. We are all very sorry for him but hope it may be for the best. Heard that the corn-yard at my early home, Meikle Geddes, has been completely burnt down and that the 'Resolute', having increased the crew to three hundred, had left St John's for the seal fishing.

April (2nd) After visiting several families on the Glenferness side of the river we called at the manager's cottage, when Mr Simpson showed us a short paragraph in the 'Scotsman' giving an account of the seal fishing near Newfoundland. We were pleased to see that the 'Resolute' had been the most successful, having secured thirty four thousand. On my way home before my husband, I met an old pauper woman from the Streens going to the village for some few things she needed. Sitting down beside her on a grassy bank, she gave me a handful of sweets and half a dozen of eggs from her little basket but let me hope that she was none the less able to deal with the merchant when she reached the shop.

May (7th) Elsie went to Inverness and bought a nice organ which we think will be a great pleasure to us all. (28th) This is my birthday. I am now forty four years old and have to acknowledge that 'Blessing and mercy have followed me all the days of my life.' Our son has now sailed for the Davies Straits whale fishing. I trust every one on board may be preserved from all danger and that the 'Resolute' may escape being 'nipped' in the ice.

June (14th) We were surprised and delighted this morning to see a pair of Goldfinches *Carduelis elegans* feeding on some dandelion seed in our garden. They can only be tourists however, that have extended their visit for a few weeks into Nairnshire, on account of the mild

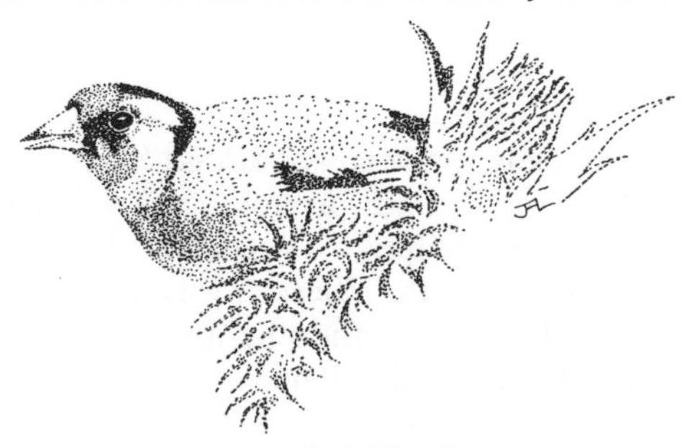

Goldfinch

weather. (17th) H.M. Inspector, with a carriageful of ladies, gave us a 'surprise' visit, examined the school registers and remained to tea. A pair of Ring-ouzels or Mountain blackbirds have been enjoying themselves among our strawberries for the last few days and we have not disturbed them.

August (7th) We were rather alarmed at mid-day by a neighbouring lassie, who come running to the schoolhouse to say that her little brother was dying from the effects of a swollen throat. On reaching the house I gave him a dose of castor oil, along with a gargle of iron, and the poor little fellow soon after began to recover. (10th) My dear husband's birthday. School children were examined in Religious Knowledge, and Mr T D Brodie of Coulmony presented a number of very handsome prizes . . . (25th) When paying a visit to the Stewart family at Aitnoch, Robert discovered a bed of the famous Grass of Parnassus *Parnassia palustrus*. This beautiful plant appears to have mistaken its habitation in this country, as it is usually found in a marshy spot and seldom on elevated grounds as might be expected. It is the only British species in its class, but why it should be called a grass, I cannot imagine.

September [No date] We visited a number of parents to-day on the east side of the river. On our way home a poor Robin Red-breast, in flying from a height, struck the upper wire of the fence along the road with great force and fell dead almost at our feet. Although I have no faith in omens, I could not help fearing the incident might be indicative that something may have befallen my dear son, who by this time should be on his return voyage from the far North. In the evening Robert took in some eighty pounds of excellent honey from our largest hive and there is much more to come.

October (4th) Received a letter from Mrs Lightbody, Jersey City, enclosing £2 for her pensioner at Burnside, Auldearn. She is very angry to have heard from himself that he has laid aside most of her former bounty in order to pay for a 'respectable' funeral! She threatens to send him no more, but we shall intercede and trust that this may not be the case.

November (4th) Greatly pleased to hear that my son has arrived safe and well at Dundee. In order, if possible, to reach Aberdeen in time for his classes, he changed places on the high sea with the surgeon on board the 'Arctic' and in this way got back a week or two earlier. He gave me a pair of Greenland slippers, lined with seal-skin as well as a 'mickie' dog's skin and a wild boar's tusk set in silver as a breast-pin. For his father, he brought a beautiful model of the Esquimaux 'kyak' along with a dozen of the 'Burgomaster's' eggs from Carey Islands in the far north of Baffin Bay. (26th) Brodie of Brodie, being a candidate to represent Elgin and Nairn in Parliament, called here with his wife Lady Eleanor and waited to drink tea with us. We hope he may be successful, although Sir George Macpherson-Grant is a strong opponent. (27th) To-night there was a splendid display of meteors for several hours after sunset. They appeared to originate near the constellation of Leo, and to form an 'umbrella of fire' above our earth. Bright and swift in their course downwards, many threw off, from their luminous tails, millions of beautifully tinted sparks which formed a special characteristic of the wonderful scene. What a lesson to us of our utter impotency in the presence of such a grand and awe-inspiring outburst of Divine power!

December (2nd) Heard that Sir George Macpherson-Grant has been returned to the House of Commons as our Member by a majority of fifty six over Brodie of Brodie. He will no doubt, prove a good Representative, but we would have preferred the latter.

1886

January (1st) Although a very quiet day I have received many presents from parents and friends. As the weather is very severe I have among my feathered callers, Rooks, Partridges as well as a poor cripple Jackdaw. This morning Robin come in at our bed-room window – a herald, let me hope, of good news in the early future – to remind me that his breakfast was somewhat later than usual. Dear birdie, he was not forgotten.

April (2nd) Very sorry to learn from the 'Scotsman' that the whaler S.S. 'Resolute' has been crushed among the ice, and afterwards went down. No lives have been lost . . .

NEWSPAPER CUTTING (Scotsman?) dated 27 March 1886.
THE WRECK OF A DUNDEE SEALER

The latest American despatches, which were landed at Queenstown yesterday morning from New York, furnish the following account of the loss of the screw-steam vessel Resolute, of 424 tons, built by A. Stephen & Son, Dundee in 1880, and owned by D. Bruce & Co., of the same place. The steamship Resolute (sealer and whaler of Dundee) was crushed in the ice off Notre Dame Bay on the 27th ult., and without the slightest warning. She parted almost immediately amidships, and sank quickly. Her crew became nearly bewildered. They numbered 330 men, and were forced to leap upon the ice, abandoning everything. They were then compelled to travel seventy miles over fields of ice. They reached land safely, except three named White, Phillips and Meglaskin, who were missed, and have not since been heard of. The despatches also state that the Resolute was commanded by the well-known sealing master, Captain Jackman, and at the time of the disaster he had captured 20,000 seals.

(18th) A poor thriftless widow who lived on the other side of school play green, was warned out by her landlord some time ago. In her straits she applied to her two sons in America, asking for a home with them. They at once agreed to her proposal and promised to send the necessary passage money. In full faith, although they seldom wrote to her, she announced a public sale which realised some thirty shillings! That evening the cheque arrived, and next morning a small waggonette took herself and a few bundles to Nairn. Throughout, she was bright and cheerful. Some months afterwards we received a letter assuring us that she arrived in comfort and found her sons kind and well to do. What a lesson to me and mine.

June (16th) Another 'visit without notice' from Her Majesty's Inspector, but everything was found in perfect order. After school hours we drove to Nairn, when my husband read a paper on the Botany of Ardclach to the local branch of the Educational Institute. There was a full attendance and all seemed interested in the various specimens of dried plants which were laid out for inspection round the room.

July (1st) Mr Smith from the Register House, Edinburgh was here on official duty and brought us a few Gulls' eggs from the Western and Shetland Islands. They will form a valued and interesting addition to our collection. (4th) This morning we received the sad news that Mr James Riach, late Schoolmaster, Fornighty, had passed away. To us he proved a very sincere friend on many occasions . . . (17th) The Nairn Literary Institute were out today for their annual drive. On the way back from the Streens via Dulsie they drove up to the Schoolhouse in four large brakes and we entertained the whole party to tea. They were all greatly pleased with our Natural History specimens of plants, eggs and insects which had been conveniently arranged in the school room previous to their arrival. On hearing that so many visitors were to be with us, my neighbours sent me lady assistants, with warm milk, butter and cream in plenty. Col. Clarke, as president, thanked me very kindly but it was a very great pleasure to us. From Aberdeen, we received a letter from Robert, enclosing a First Class Certificate for one of his medical classes and stating that he had passed Chemistry. In the evening we all dined at the Established House.

August (8th) When dressing to go to church in the morning I observed a rash on my face and neck. To our surprise it gradually developed as a clear symptom of measles which, for a few days, made me rather sick and uncomfortable. The Ring-ouzels have come back on a visit to our garden again, and I hope they may do so for some time yet before going south.

September . . . (3rd) This week we paid our annual visit to Whitemire, and as on former occasions were treated with the utmost kindness. After dinner we drove over to Darnaway Castle with Mrs Rose, and spent the evening with a few friends who had come to meet us. Before leaving our party assembled in Randolph's Hall, where we all sang the hundredth psalm which had a most beautiful effect in that spacious apartment. Got home about midnight loaded with many good things. On arriving I found that two of my pupils had gathered a large basketful of cranberries and left them for me with our neighbour Janet Macbean. (6th) The trustees of the Lethen school, at their last meeting, did a very popular act in appointing Miss Nigella Lockhart a former parishioner, to their school at Fornighty, in room of the late teacher, who was practically dismissed for professional impudence . . .

October (8th) This forenoon the children had a delightful walk along the Findhorn with Masters Randall and Willie Clunas, who made several beautiful sketches of the river scenery near Daltra. While they were away I had a note from Achagour inviting us all to dinner in the evening. (15th) Tonight my son read a paper on his 'Arctic Experiences' to the Nairn Literary Institute [see Appendix]. The hall was crowded and he received no end of praise from the President, Colonel Clarke of Achraidh and other speakers. (20th) Our favourite cat, 'Neddie', which has been away in the wilds for some time on his own account, was yesterday found dead in a snare at the river side. We were all very sorry to hear of the sad end which had befallen our unfortunate pussy. Mr Willie Clunas sent me [a] nice watercolour sketch of Logie Bridge with Elsie in the foreground.

December (20th) For some days, Uncle has been rather out of his usual and we had to sit up with him at night. In addition to a good depth of snow, there is a rather severe frost, and I have a poor Rook with only one leg, as a frequent claimant among my feathered pensioners. A letter came today from Mrs Lightbody containing an order for two pounds to the old man James Steel at Burnside, Lethen. From a Statement recently made by Robert to the Post Master General in London, we are pleased to learn from his reply that there is to be a local letter carrier from Belivat to Dulsie three times a week which will be a great boon to that outlying district.

1887

January (1st) Had a number of friends calling on us today. I received a great many new year's gifts, and 'my cup overflows'. (16th) Heard this afternoon of the sudden death of Alexander Scott, a very promising pupil. We both went over to Glenferness in the evening to sympathize with the sorrowing parents. The roads were exceedingly slippery and in consequence, we returned rather tired but greatly pleased that we had called. (22nd) As Robert had to go down to Burnside with Mrs Lightbody's donation, I went along with him to see the Riach family before their departure for Colorado in the United States and got the last of many, many bottles of cream. (26th) By request of several friends my husband read our son's paper on his 'Arctic Experiences' while on board the S.S. 'Resolute', to a large audience in the Free Church here, and everyone seemed much interested . . .

March (10th) The Curlews, Lapwings, and Pickie-tar Gulls [Black-headed Gulls] have now returned to their summer quarters among our hills and lochs. Their well-known cries give quite a spring character to the advancing year . . . (16th) Received a letter from our son announcing that he has passed two of his medical examinations with first class honours. We noticed in the 'Scotsman' that he is third on the List of those why got certificates and prizes.

April (6th) The weather is very cold and unseasonable. Among my feathered friends I had a Mavis, a Reed-bunting and a Titlark at their morning meal. Poor little birdies, the storm has sadly interfered with their domestic arrangements, but let us hope we shall have more pleasant days in the near future . . .

Ardclach School Log Book: 18 May – Ten boys and ten girls present. Inspector's Report – . . . no grant can be allowed for the past year as the school has not been opened the required number of times. It is stated on Form IX that 'severe weather did not admit of more than 395 openings, but my Lords are unable to accept this as bringing the case under Exception ii to Article 19; seeing that the school only required to be opened on 200 days (400 openings) during the whole year' . . . In August the log book was called up by the Department who eventually agreed to pay the grant. 'They will expect any deficiency of school openings unavoidably caused at one season to be compensated as far as possible by restricting to some extent other holidays.' The grant amounted to £36.5s.

June (9th) Robert and I called on a number of sick people today and they were all very pleased to see us. We walked home by the river side amid a profusion of flowers and ferns which would have delighted any Botanist. On our arrival I found that a kind friend had sent me a couple of hares and a large cut of a fine salmon. When Elsie was at Achagour today helping Mrs Rose and McPherson with some household arrangement, to their great surprise Mr James Mackillican walked in from Calcutta! (16th) We are pleased to find that a dear Partridge has built her nest in our garden on a sunny bank, just inside the fence along the school road and within some four yards from the play-ground gate. Any passer-by who knows the spot may look right down on the trustful hen which is wonderfully protected by the similarity of her plumage to the natural surroundings of withered grass and brown soil. We are deeply interested in this rare confidence and hope that she may be able without mishap, to develop her cherished treasures in due course, and that her offspring may be all preserved from the sportsman's gun during the approaching shooting season. (20th) A pretty Yellowhammer somewhat thoughtlessly flew into the schoolroom today and in its fear, dashed itself so forcibly against the window panes that it fell on the floor quite stunned. I took it up, and after holding it in my hand for a short time, was pleased to see it fly away.

July . . . (19th) Robert and I drove to Torrich, and afterwards went with the Macpherson family to the Cawdor Flower Show. It was really delightful to meet so many old and dear friends. On our return we sat down to a sumptuous supper, and the clock struck three the next morning before we left for home! Mrs Macpherson loaded me with several prize exhibits – butter, eggs and cheese. (25th) Mr and Mrs Jamieson, teachers, Nairn, with her sister from Edinburgh, were here. In the afternoon we all had tea on a grassy haugh at the river side, under the spreading branches of a fine old rowan tree which was loaded with large clusters of red fruit. The weather was lovely, while the floral display was unimpaired along the banks and we all enjoyed the picnic to the full.

September (4th) This is our Silver Wedding Day, but, Alas!, how many of the friends, who were bright and happy at our marriage, have passed away and joined the majority. At breakfast my husband and I had a very pleasant surprise. Robert and Elsie, at no little sacrifice on their part, presented a valuable brooch to me and a beautiful Aneroid Barometer to their father. Both articles were procured with great

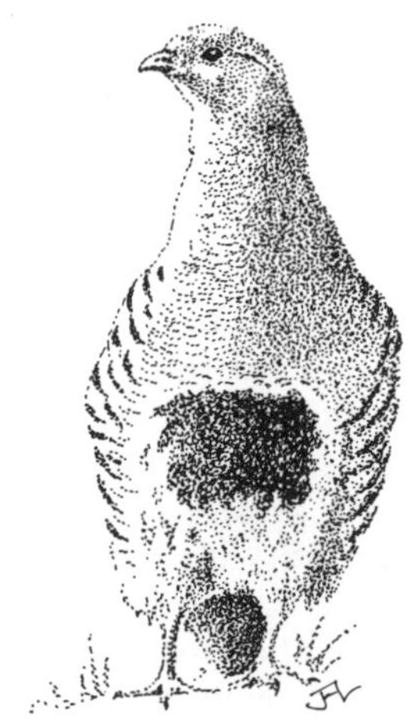

Partridge

secrecy through the post office from Edinburgh, and we very highly esteem the filial spirit which prompted them to do this . . .

October (2nd) Uncle has been in bed all day. He is complaining of what seems to be a continued attack of bile. (14th) As my husband had to read a Paper on 'The Flora of Ardclach' to the Literary Institute, we got the Achagour pony, and drove down to Nairn on a bitterly cold afternoon. Most of the way he went at a very easy trot, but when within some fifty yards of Tradespark, where we were to put up, 'Comet' suddenly came down on the road and broke both the trams! – The brute, we were told, had fallen asleep. Neither of us however, was in the least hurt, for which we were very thankful. At the meeting, Col. Clarke presided over a large attendance and all the after speakers referred to us both in very complimentary terms. (23rd) A decent pauper having died at Logie Bridge, we went over in the evening to sympathize with the relatives and held a short service before leaving. While on our way home, a very heavy shower of rain came on and having no umbrella, we got quite drenched. (28th) The coach-builder has now sent up the damaged trap with a new pair of trams at a cost of £2–6s. Mr James Mackillican being about to return to India, Robert and I were asked to dinner when we met several old acquaintances and spent a very pleasant evening.

Ardclach School Log Book: October – 30 pupils enrolled but on 21st a few were still at field labour, and on 28th a few were still at potatoes.

December

Ardclach School Log Book: (9th) Taught during play hour, as roads difficult, with a threatening of another fall of snow, and dismissed at 3 o'clock today.

. . . (17th) The weather is still cold and cheerless. Uncle who has been entirely confined to bed for the last few days, rose at midnight and tried to go out, but fortunately failed to open the outer door. (22nd) This morning he sank very low but rallied until the evening when he passed peacefully away at five o'clock. None of us was in church but after the sermon a number of friends called and held a short service in the schoolhouse. (26th) Uncle was buried today in Geddes Church Yard. He would have completed his ninetieth year had he lived to the following April.

1888

January (11th) Last night a huge meteorite appeared to fall in a field near the schoolhouse. The nucleus and its relative train were of surpassing brilliance and lighted up the district for a few seconds to a noontide clearness. These strange bodies dash at an enormous speed into our upper atmosphere, with the result that, in their onward progress through it, they become intensely heated and usually get burnt up. It would be interesting to know how much, if any, solid matter remained by the time this special one reached the earth. (18th) For some days past my health has been considerably below par. I have very little desire for food and no will to make the least exertion. Elsie has taken my place in school and the children never forget to ask for me as they are leaving at four o'clock.

Ardclach School Log Book: Measles and colds reduced attendances. Assistant Mistress off due to illness.

(22nd) The weather has become fresh and pleasant. I had a lovely sleep last night and now feel much better. A number of friends have been calling to see me and brought many dainties which, for some time, I was unable to enjoy. Rachel sent me from Glenferness, a bunch of forced rhubarb, along with a bottle of thick cream which I relished exceedingly.

February (2nd) While in bed this morning we felt a distinct shock of horizontal earthquake. On the Ferness side of the Findhorn the tremour, which lasted for a few seconds, rattled the dishes in all the cupboards, and stopped the various clocks at four a.m. We were deeply impressed with our absolute helplessness in the presence of such a terrible force.

March (8th) Although snow still lingers in small patches, the Lapwings and Curlews have returned to Ardclach and the bees were out in great numbers at mid-day. After school Robert went over to Glenferness to visit the sick people. (27th) Another fall of snow. My feathered pensioners have again come back to solicit a few crumbs and are most attentive when I shake the table-cloth at the door. Elsie has finished a knitted bed-cover on which she has been working at odd times for over a year. (20th) This morning we heard with deep sorrow that our friend Mr William Rose, Farmer, Achindown, died, after having been married for only a few months. The election of the School Board took place today. By a careful manipulation of the cumulative vote the district on the east side of the river has returned a majority of members and, as a result, the Ferness people expect that the Parish School will be transferred very soon to the village.

Ardclach School Log Book: School Board – John Robertson (Chairman), Rev. D. Miller, Rob. Walker (Forres), John Grigor (Coulmony), P. Mackillican (Achagour), Rev. A Macdonald.

May (12th) In looking over an American newspaper I was very sorry to observe the death of our good friend Mrs Lightbody of Jersey City on the 21st March last. In the evening Robert and I called on a few invalids and, let me hope, that we helped to relieve for a little, the dull monotony of the sick chamber. (19th) Mrs Campbell, Moss-side, sent me, as she often does, a large pailful of warm milk but in this case some three dozen of 'Pickie-tars' eggs from the Loch of Belivat.

June (2nd) In the afternoon Robert and I called at Achavrate to see Miss Macdonald, who is very poorly. She does not expect to recover but is cheerful and happy. Her brother, Duncan drove us home during a heavy fall of snow which accumulated on the surface and lay for a few hours to the depth of fully an inch. Such a state of weather at this season must be very discouraging for farmers. (9th) A brother of Mr Mackintosh, Score, who is on a visit to his native parish, came here today to look over the old school where he received his early education under the late Henry Mackintosh. He told us that he still retained many pleasant memories of those bygone days and his youthful exploits with like-minded companions, now dead or scattered all over the world . . . (19th) Our son has entered on his duties as assistant to Dr Gilmour at Linlithgow. (23rd) In a letter of yesterday we regret to learn that he is not at all satisfied with his prospects and may leave very soon.

September (4th) This is the anniversary of our marriage – a union which has been, in every respect, a very happy one to us both. (6th) At the request of Mr Gordon, Dentist, Inverness. Robert delivered his lecture on 'The Flora of Ardclach' and exhibited specimens of dried plants to the local Gardeners' Association in the Free Library. The Gordon family were exceedingly kind and did everything in their power to make our visit as pleasant as possible . . . (17th) At the School Board meeting today it was decided, by a majority, that we are to be transferred to Ferness. The Earl of Leven and Melville has undertaken to bear all the expenses in connection with the new building and internal alterations. (19th) Our friends Mr and Mrs Gordon (Dentist) and James Fraser, Esq. (19th) C.E. came from Inverness and spent the day with us. After dinner the gentlemen had a pleasant walk along the Findhorn, and by the time they returned, Mrs Gordon, Elsie and I had tea set for them as a surprise, on a grassy haugh under a rowan tree at a lovely spot on the river bank. The weather being perfect we all enjoyed our little picnic to the full.

Ardclach School Log Book: October – Late harvest and attendance irregular.

November . . . (14th) This is Miss Carrie Murdoch's marriage day and we were all at Lynemore. For the season, the weather was delightful. There was a large and brilliant gathering of relations, friends and neighbours. The bride looked well and was dressed in a white Indian silk – the gift of Mr James Mackillican of Calcutta. After the ceremony the party sat down to a sumptuous feast and everyone enjoyed the occasion to the utmost. We hope that Mr and Mrs Marr may have a long and very happy life.

December (18th) A Commissioner from the Education department was here in regard to the proposed transfer of our school to the Glenferness side of the Parish.

1889

January (8th) The snow has been drifting into huge wreaths and only a few children were able to be in school. As the railway is completely blocked on the higher portions, no mails have arrived for some days and we feel ourselves shut out from the world, but we have abundant stores as well as many comforts for which we desire to be very thankful. My poor birdies are again calling on me. In addition to their usual crumbs I gave them a large bone with both fat and marrow. This pleased them greatly.

Ardclach School Log Book: Rev. David Miller gave 2s. to be given, 1s. to the best boy and 1s. to the best girl in School – the choice to be left to themselves. Jeannie Munro and William were voted the most deserving.

March (2nd) This morning Robert posted a letter to Gilbert Fraser Esq., Her Britannic Majesty's Consul-General, New York (a Nairn loon) regarding the late Mrs Lightbody's Will . . . (17th) In answer to his New York communication Robert received the following:-

Her Britannic Majesty's Consulate General, New York, 4th April 1889.

> *Dear Sir – In reply to your letter of the 2nd ultimo, I beg to inform you that I have ascertained that the late Mrs Janet Lightbody of Jersey City, in the State of New Jersey, has bequeathed to the Ardclach School Board the sum of $2500 – about £500 – to be know as the 'Lightbody Endowment', and to be invested by them, and the interest used as a Bursary for boys.*
>
> *I am, dear Sir, yours faithfully. G. Fraser.* First British Vice-Consul.

(20th) My husband has written to the Chairman of our Board informing him of the bequest. He stated that, being [contacted] by Mrs Lightbody in the autumn of 1882 regarding a legacy to the parish of her late husband, he had suggested to her the propriety of leaving £550 for free education to the children . . . He hoped that the interest of the sum now announced would prove a great benefit to not a few deserving boys, for all time coming, in the parish. (23rd) To this the Chairman replied – 'Your letter is very gratifying, and you deserve the thanks of all interested in the education of the parish for the part you have played. Yours faithfully, J.S. Robertson.'

May (2nd) Tonight Robert has gone with a few voters, to dine at Mid-Fleenas where they are to meet Brodie of Brodie, the Conservative Parliamentary Candidate for Elgin and Nairn at the next general election. (23rd) Our pussy 'Don' returned from his hunting ground last night with a very sore paw. It had been for the second time in a trap, but thanks to the keeper, he had once more been let off . . .

June (4th) The School Report has now come and we are both very thankful to find that it is an excellent one. (15th) In the afternoon, we went by the foot path, along the rocky side of the Findhorn as far as Daltra. It would be hard to find a walk more solitary, and at the same time more exciting to the mind at every step. The little birds, amid a profusion of leaves and flowers, were busy attending to their recently hatched fledglings. Resting on a tiny blossom, I found a beautifully marked moth *Amphydasis betularia*, which proved to be new to Robert's collection, and he is very proud of it. Mr John Rose, the farmer, is much failed since we last saw him, but kind and hospitable as ever. Alexander, his son, gave me a fine salmon which he caught only a few minutes before our arrival . . .

July (10th) . . . Heard from our son that he has gained an honours medical certificate. A few days ago, 'Don' took in a poor disabled Lapwing and this forenoon he came home with a fine grouse, and proudly laid it down at my feet. I wish in future, he would give less attention to toads, newts and shrews, rats, voles and weasels, and present me, from time to time, with captures which, like this, would be greatly more appreciated . . . (18th) This is the local Communion fast day and we both dined at the Free Church manse. The School Board has resolved to sell the property here, together with the school and schoolhouse at Fornighty, after the necessary three months' notice to the teacher, Miss Lockhart. (26th) In a letter from Robert, we have the good news that he has passed the final examination in medicine, and is now M.B.; C.M. (27th) Elsie has gone to Aberdeen to see her brother capped. We are getting many congratulations. (29th) Mr (now Professor) Cosmo Hill Burton called today with a strange caterpillar, *Dicranura vinula*, which he found feeding on the leaves of *Populus tremula* at the river side and was greatly struck with its grotesque shape and beautiful colouring.

August (19th) Received intimation that through Captain Bain (Nairn) of the S.S. 'Clan Mackintosh', Robert has been appointed surgeon of the S.S 'Matheson' from Liverpool to Calcutta. In the evening my two Roberts dined at Achagour, where they met Colonel Matheson, an Ardersier 'loon'. He is now Inspector General of the British fortresses. (28th) Early this morning we took our places on the S.S. 'Earnholm' for a sea trip along with the Nairn Literary Institute to Dunrobin and Cromarty. Met a number of nice people on board and was much interested in the sailors and the way they did their work. All day there was a strong land breeze, which caused a good deal of pitching and tossing. A few were sick but, as I thought, the gale only added to the pleasure of our excursion. Being considerably delayed by a head wind, the Castle and grounds had to be viewed through binoculars, as there was no time to land. At Cromarty however, we had about an hour ashore, which we spent in visiting Hugh Miller's early home, his monument on the rising ground above the town and the old Church yard where he met the young lady who afterwards became his wife. From the long exposure my face was greatly sunburnt but I enjoyed the day's outing to the full.

September (17th) All being well, our son sailed from Liverpool today. The 'Matheson', as a high class steamer, is one of those reserved by Government for war purposes in the event of need. Most of the crew are lascars but the captain and other officials are British. (19th) This morning the Earl of Leven and Melville met with a rather serious accident. After leaving Glenferness for London, the horses took fright on the way to Forres and he was thrown from his carriage. He was very much bruised and cut about the face. We see by the newspaper that Brodie of Brodie died a day or two ago in the south of Europe. He will be deeply regretted over Nairnshire.

October (1st) Everyone is pleased to hear, although it is hope against hope, that there is a fair chance of the Earl's ultimate recovery. Robert has arrived at Port Said where he is experiencing all the fierceness of tropical heat. Today the sky was cloudless and the air pure and vigorous, but at night there were thunder and lightning while the rain fell in sheets . . . (22nd) Lord Leven died today. The Glenferness tenants will never get a more considerate landlord. (28th) Poor 'Don' after being away for more than a week has come home with a very sore paw, but the bone is not broken. Once again some kind friend was let him out of a trap.

November (1st) We find by the 'Scotsman' that the 'Clan Matheson' has left Calcutta for London. This morning the Ferness scholars very proudly brought me a large salmon which they found stranded at the river side near the suspension bridge. It had probably been killed by an otter. Although it weighed upwards of twenty pounds and seemed quite fresh, we buried it in the garden. Last night my husband read a paper on 'The Legends of Ardclach' to the Nairn Literary Institute.

December (7th) Yesterday, our neighbour, Alexander Gordon, Dalnaheglis, met with a serious accident. Slipping on the edge of a rocky crag some eighty feet above the river, he fell down almost to the bottom and broke his thigh bone. Some hours afterwards, by tracing his foot-prints on a thin covering of snow, he was discovered and carefully raised to the summit by a number of men with ropes and bags. We hope he may have a good recovery. (25th) Spent a quiet, but very happy Christmas. In the evening we received by post a number of cards and a beautiful plaque painted for me by Miss Jeannie Lockhart, Fornighty. It is quite a gem and I appreciate her gift very highly. (30th) This is our dear son's birthday. By telegram from Glasgow we learn that he has engaged to return to India with the 'Clan Matheson'.

1890

January (1st) Spent the day very pleasantly with Mrs Lockhart and warmly congratulated her on the unexpected appointment of her daughter Nigella to reopen the [Fornighty] school which had been purchased by the Lethen family for the benefit of the district. (9th) A most enthusiastic meeting was held by the local rate-payers to thank Mr Brodie, and welcome their former teacher back from Castleton, Thurso . . .

February (6th) In a letter from Malta, Robert states that his ship encountered a terrible gale when in the Bay of Biscay. They were driven far off their usual course along the Spanish coast, and lost their cow and several sheep. For a time the captain had great doubts whether the 'Matheson' would be able to weather the storm. (14th) There is a good deal of snow on the ground with intense frost and a great many of our scholars are unable to be in school on account of colds and influenza . . .

March (3rd) Observed by the newspapers that the steamship 'Quetta' has gone down in Torres Straits, near Cape York, with the loss of 164 persons. Among those drowned we are sorry to see the name of David Rose, the chief engineer, an old Cawdor scholar who lived at Viewhill. The School Board has now arranged that we are to be transferred to Ferness sometime before the first of August next. In a letter from our son, he states that there is a number of patients aboard, and that an Indian officer's wife gave birth to a daughter on mid-ocean between Malta and Gibraltar.

May (14th) An interesting pair of Storm cocks *Turdus viscivorous* have built their nest in the bushy top of a pine tree near our house. In all their nuptial duties it is evident that both birds are devotedly attached to each other. Should any poor Lapwing, gull or Jackdaw inadvertently chance to fly past in the near vicinity, the male bird at once darts from his retreat, and vigorously attacks, again and again,

Mistle Thrush

the astonished passer-by until it has managed to place itself at such a distance that further hostility is considered unnecessary. In the morning when our 'Don' goes out on his official rounds, the cock is sure to observe him and, swooping down to the nearest point consistent with personal safety, pours out, in bird language, a storm of the most insulting invective against him and all his kin. 'Don', instead of taking it seriously to heart, treats the whole matter with the utmost indifference, although by an occasional side glance he watches for his calumniator to come within springing distance when, without doubt, the abuse would very quickly be brought to a close at the expense of poor Mr *Turdus*.

(20th) About ten o'clock at night, a strange man, rather over middle age, in good but somewhat faded attire came to the door and asked for a bed. He had on neither collar nor tie, and the skin of his open breast was quite bronzed with the sun. He was a brother, he said, of the late Rev. Colin Mackenzie, and just home on a visit from Australia. On his way here he had been at the Free Church manse and, though after full explanations, he had handed to the lady eight sovereigns for the poor of the congregation, she still declined to admit him. He thereafter called at the Established Manse and gave the minister the same sum for a like purpose, but was assured that there was no spare room, as the house was in the hands of workmen and undergoing extensive repairs. Being equally unsuccessful at the farm of Levrattich, he would be thankful, he said, to sleep on a 'shake down' in my kitchen. After some hesitation, I took him in and gave him our best bedroom. While I was preparing some supper he told us that he was a graduate of King's College, Aberdeen and in evidence repeated several odes from Horace. Then as he was relating many of his rough experiences as a bushman, he handed me two sovereigns from a well-worn hempen bag, to be awarded as prizes for good conduct among our scholars.

Next morning, he visited the Church yard and burying place of his late brother and, before leaving to walk to Nairn, thanked me very kindly, and promised on his return from abroad, to come and see us in our new home at Ferness. I was glad that I had given the poor man a bed but, O, his appearance was very misleading. (24th) Her Majesty's Inspector examined the Knockandhu scholars along with ours and although everyone, as usual, did very well, I had to go to bed in the afternoon with a severe nervous headache. Mr Macleod and Miss Penny [teacher at Knockandhu school with 16 scholars] waited to dinner.

June (3rd) Our son has got an appointment as medical assistant to Dr MacGowan, Bellshill, near Glasgow. Elsie was looking over our new house at Ferness and thinks it will be very convenient when finished. (12th) In a letter from Robert, we are pleased to hear that he is greatly pleased with the new sphere of his labour. (18th) In addition to several local presents during the past few days, I have got a valuable Cashmere shawl and pretty brooch from Mr Moir in Bombay who has come to stay with us for some time. (21st) The Education Department, having called in my husband's Parchment Certificate, has now returned it raised to the First Class. (29th) When walking today with Mr Moir in the Dulsie Wood, Robert discovered a delightfully fragrant plant which turns out to be the *Linnaea borealis.* Though very common in Scandinavia it is rare in Great Britain, being occasionally found in elevated fir woods which are not very favourable to plant life in general. So far as we know, this is the only station, which was hitherto unknown, in Nairnshire. As the name implies it is called after the Father of Botany [the Swede Carl von Linné] who selected this humble growth as the medium by which he desired his name to be transmitted to posterity, because he thought its modest appearance and lowly habits were the most fitting emblems of his own early condition.

July (25th) Before dismissing the children in the afternoon we told the story of Mr Mackenzie's visit from Australia and surprised them by spreading out, at his expense, a nice tea, and thereafter distributed rewards for progress and good conduct. (28th) The Ardclach Parish School was permanently closed today and we all feel very sorry. I trust we may be as happy in our new home at Ferness as we have been here.

Ardclach School Log Book: Gave the autumn holidays, after which the present staff will meet the children in Ferness school, the Ardclach school being now closed.

NAIRNSHIRE TELEGRAPH 30 July 1890

Presentation and opening of new school at Ferness.

On Saturday a new school with teacher's house, garden and

Twinflower

playground, in the village of Ferness, were handed over to the Ardclach School Board by the Earl of Leven and Melville. The occasion was regarded as of peculiar interest in the district and a large number of the people in the neighbourhood assembled to witness the proceedings.

The teacher's house is a handsome building. It faces the village street and although not new, it has been so thoroughly renovated, improved and enlarged, that it is as good as new. The school lies immediately behind the teacher's house and it is somewhat to be regretted that so fine a school should be so completely concealed from the passer-by. It is not large, though large enough probably for the district. It has two classrooms and these have been admirably fitted up. The ventilation, lighting, and seating have been carried out on the most approved principles and the whole equipment of the school is of the most complete description. The windows are filled in with stained glass of a very pretty shade. The north window might with advantage have been full length, as the main classroom requires a little more light, but this will probably be effected if found necessary. One feature is the excellent water supply to the school and the provision for the children washing their hands before entering the classrooms.

The Earl of Leven and Melville arrived punctually at the hour and as this is the first time his Lordship has appeared in a public capacity since his accession to the title and estates, he received a most cordial reception.

The Earl of Leven, we may be permitted to say here, is a comparatively young man, very handsome, and intellectual looking. He speaks with ease and fluency and impresses everyone with his desire to deal justly and generously. Although owning property in Nairnshire for some time back, the Earl's predecessors unfortunately took no part in the public business of the county, but it is hoped that Lord Leven's public appearance at Ferness on Saturday will be the beginning of a change in this respect and that the family of Leven and Melville will be more associated with the district than hitherto.

CHAPTER 6

A Flitting to Ferness

July (30th) Our furniture and other goods have now been removed by the local farmers without a single mishap. In the evening James and Donald Rose, along with Rachel, helped us to arrange a few things in the various rooms. Before leaving we had supper and some music, which we concluded by singing the Old Hundred to its own psalm.

August (2nd) This afternoon my husband visited all the neighbours and was gratified to find that our removal to Ferness had given general satisfaction. A great many friends from both sides of the river have been calling on us, and my pantry is quite full of all sorts of dainty things. Goodness and Mercy are surely following us here also. (9th) My husband and I had a run to Aberdeen on a visit to Mr Moir and his mother who is now rather frail. A few days later we drove up to the Braes of Midmar to see Robert's cousin, Hannah and his aunt Janet, an old lady in her ninetieth year. We found her wonderfully well and even able to do lots of little things in her room. Our good friend one evening took us to the theatre – the first time for me – but I did not think the play was worth one third of the price that was paid for our enjoyment. Before leaving Aberdeen we bought over thirty pounds worth of new furniture for the Ferness schoolhouse. (20th) This was a specially happy day. We had Mr and Mrs Rose, Nairn; Mr and Mrs Fraser (Banker, London), and six other of their friends here at luncheon and tea. As the day was all that could be desired the party drove home by Lynemore where they were all charmed with the kindness and winning courtesy of our good friend Mrs Murdoch.

September (2nd) By this evening's post we received a letter from Miss Cunningham, Free Church Manse, Grangemouth, with some specimens of the famous Edelweiss *Gnaphalium leontopodium*, which she gathered last summer for Robert on its native rocks in Switzerland. This is the well known bridal flower, and is a sweet little blossom. The whole plant is thickly covered with long white woolly hairs and is much prized by Botanists. It can only be procured at some personal risk among the Alps after reaching a height of over five thousand feet. (4th) Another anniversary of our happy marriage. (15th) Began work in our new school with twenty six children. May God give us Grace and Health to perform our duties aright as long as we may be called upon to discharge them here.

Ferness School Log Book: 15 September – Ferness Public School opened 'being more centrally situated with regard to the population than the Ardclach School'.

October (18th) Being in Forres yesterday, my husband called at the coach-builder's and ordered a new dog-cart, that I may get a drive to the church on Sundays. (23rd) A very sad affair happened this afternoon. Mr Alexander Rose, Farmer, Tomnarroch, when on his way with a restive pony to meet his wife, was thrown out of his trap among some loose stones at the roadside on the New Inn brae. After he was discovered, the Urquharts, Logie Bridge, laid him on a chaff bed and conveyed him home in a cart. Several of his ribs were broken and the sharp ends having penetrated the lungs, he swelled and died two hours after the mishap. Mrs Urquhart and I dressed the remains. He was a kindly old man and much respected. (28th) The other day a middle-aged man, in decent attire, called at the shop beside us and produced a beautiful lady's ring, set, he observed, with a couple of diamonds and the same number of rubies. He had just found it he added, on the road near by and believed it had been lost by some gallant young man who had intended it as a present for his sweetheart in the district. Being of no use to the finder, he wished to leave it in the hope that the lad would turn up in a few days and have it restored. As an after-thought, he naively suggested that he was fairly entitled to a few shillings of a reward which, no doubt, would be willingly refunded by the loser, and if not, the holder herself would become the possessor of a costly piece of jewellery for a mere trifle. The artifice proved successful; the rogue got five shillings, and the precious gem turned out to be only a pretty but worthless trinket.

November . . . (14th) Our new dog-cart was sent up from Forres to-day and we are very well pleased with it. (15th) Ladies Sophia and Florence Leslie-Melville called to look over Robert's natural history specimens and had tea with us before leaving.

December (6th) Our other cat, 'Daisy', which could not be found on the afternoon of our removal from the Ardclach Schoolhouse, was to-day sent over in a basket by a late neighbour who observed her sitting in the window after dark. When the lid was lifted she came out and at once made friends with us – clinging to my dress and sitting on Robert's knee by turns. She took to her new home as contentedly as if she had been living in it from kittenhood. During the last four months, in the midst of traps and snares, with keepers and dogs to boot, her existence among the wilds has been little short of a miracle. (31st) On the occasion of the new farm square being finished, we all dined in the afternoon with a large party of friends at Achagour. Then in the evening Mr James Mackillican entertained to supper and a dance, his own servants along with the various tradesmen who had been engaged on the work.

1891

January (2nd) We were very sorry this morning to hear that Professor Cosmo Innes Burton, a young man of great promise, died some time ago at Shanghai of malignant smallpox, after a few days' illness. I have written a letter of sympathy to his poor mother and sister in the time of their sad affliction.

Ferness School Log Book: 5 January – Began a scheme today of giving a cup of coffee to the children at midday. 23 January – Poor light in the schoolroom.

March (14th) To-day Robert had a long and interesting letter from Mr James Mackenzie, Partick, one of the first scholars who came to school after his appointment to Cawdor Free Church Institution there in 1858. He remembers him as a very poor but diligent boy who never required to be pressed to do his work. As the result he now occupies a highly responsible and lucrative position in the employment of one of the largest commercial firms in the great metropolis of the west.

April (14th) The Census papers were all returned to the School-house to-day and from them we now find that our parish contains 991 souls including, however, 31 tinkers who were found camping for the night on the moor at Highland Boath while on their way to Geddes Market. One old couple insisted that their ages should be recorded as sixty because they were each born in the same year as the battle of Waterloo was fought! By the 15th of May next the two detached portions of our parish locally situated in the county of Elgin will be added, along with 49 inhabitants, to the parish of Edenkillie. The exact number therefore, in Ardclach will be 991 minus (31 + 49) or 911 which shows a decrease of 206 since the former census, (1117) in the year 1881. Two hundred and five in the parish can speak both Gaelic and English while there is only one aged female who can use the Celtic alone. ((21st) Yesterday a neighbour of ours while arranging some boxes on his cart near Forres, accidentally slipped and fell headlong on the road. On reaching home in a very weakly condition, Robert and I dressed his wounds and removed several small stones which had got embedded in the flesh. We hope that with rest and good nursing he will be able in a few weeks to attend to his usual duties.

May (19th) We are very sorry to hear that Mr Simon Mackenzie, our erratic visitor from Australia, has not been able to leave Sydney for this country on account of ill health.

Ferness School Log Book: May – 20 boys and 24 girls at school.

June (23rd) Our friends the Clunas family, when wintering in Tangiers, sent Robert a box containing a few very good specimens of native locusts, dragon-flies and beetles. Among them was the shell of the Strawberry crab *Eurynome asper*. It was found on the African side of the Straits in rather deep water and has a wonderful adaptation to its natural environment. The back is studded with numerous conical excrescences sufficiently red to suggest the likeness to the garden fruit and hence the name. I too, got additions to my domestic cabinet – cream, butter, eggs and cheese, for which I am grateful.

July (26th) Very sorry to hear that our late neighbour, Mr John MacNaughton, parish teacher, died yesterday at Cawdor, after a rather short illness. In school, though a somewhat severe disciplinarian, he devoted himself unsparingly to his professional duties and turned out a number of clever boys who, in many cases, rose to good positions all over the world. Among congenial friends he was exceedingly humorous and always entered with great zest into the spirit of any amusing anecdote or other favourite subject. (30th) There is to be a meeting of the Northern Scientific Societies in Nairn to-morrow night and my husband has been asked to take down his collection of Insects and Plants, as an illustration of the natural history of the county.

September (2nd) Had Sir William Cameron Gull at tea. He wishes to represent the united counties of Elgin and Nairn in Parliament and we hope he may be returned at the next general election. (4th) This is the twenty ninth anniversary of our marriage which we both feel sure was the best move in our life because Goodness and Mercy have continued to follow us hitherto. (9th) From a thoughtless act our wood-pile was set on fire at the end of the school. Fortunately it was discovered in time, otherwise the whole place would have been burned to the ground.

1892

January (1st) This was a very happy New Year's day. My husband was paid his Registration salary and I had several presents including a handsome cheque from my son. 'A Window in Thrums', and 'Auld Licht Idylls' Barrie came from a friend in Glasgow and we had lots of callers during the day. We see from the newspaper that our neighbour, Mr T.D. Brodie, Dunearn, has been created a Baronet and that the Rev Adam Macleod, Free Church minister of Croy, died this morning.

Ferness School Log Book: 8 January – 18 inches of snow, school closed mid-month.

(11th) A great deal of snow has recently fallen and, as the depth must now average fully twenty inches in a dry powdery condition, the roads are all but impossible. Old Mrs Cameron, Ballintore, was buried to-day, and the friends and neighbours had an unusual experience. Several farmers on horseback rode in the morning, one after the other, from the house to the church-yard in order to make a footpath. Before 'lifting', the coffin was suspended lengthwise from a pole some thirteen feet long and thus carried on the shoulders between two or four men in a line. When the bearers became exhausted, their places were taken by a relay from those immediately behind while they stepped aside and stood among the untrodden snow till the file of mourners had passed and then fell into line till their turn in due course, came round again. Mrs Cameron lived a very retired life but was a good Christian woman. She was the last in the parish who continued to wear on all occasions a close old fashioned linen cap of spotless white. (29th) A rapid thaw has now set in and the streams are in full flood. The current in the Findhorn to-day is slightly overflowing the floor of the iron bridge at the Established Church, thus carrying down a greater volume of water at a time than has been observed for many years past.

February . . . (11th) Sorry to hear that Col. Grant of Househill died yesterday. After honourable service in India, he struck across equatorial Africa from the east coast and, along with Captain Speke (1860–63), explored the great lakes at the sources of the Nile. In this way he opened up a country which was previously unknown and so added greatly to our knowledge of the Dark Continent. (12th) We were all greatly troubled this morning to have the sad news that our dear friend Mrs Rose, Whitemire, had been called away from this earthly scene . . .

March (5th) At play-time the scholars were greatly excited to-day in having captured 'an awful' big weasel', *Mustela putorius* [polecat], on the bank of the Findhorn. Each one being armed with a switch of brush wood, it was successfully driven from an old rabbit's hole in which it had taken refuge and after a 'terrible' onslaught of kicks, slashings, and tramping of feet, the poor 'foumart' at last fell dead from a stroke aimed at a venture. It was then carried home and proudly laid on the 'maister's' desk to show what his boys could when they got the chance. (28th) Last night I was fondling a tiny lamb, the firstling of a flock on the pasture near here. Poor wee thing! Although it came to the world in bitterly cold weather, its heartless mother left it bleating piteously on the bare moor and could nowhere be found. (30th) Very pleased to learn that our old Cawdor scholar, Captain William Cameron, has been appointed Chief Constable of Partick, an important suburb of Glasgow.

April (6th) To our great surprise a deputation from the Young Men's Association called at the schoolhouse in the evening and presented me with a beautiful silver-plated Cake Basket on which is inscribed:- 'Presented to Mrs Thomson by the Members of the Ardclach Young Men's Association as a mark of Esteem, April 1892'.

I am very proud of the gift but appreciate still more the spirit that prompted it. (8th) My husband and I were present this afternoon at a very interesting marriage at the Score farm, where Mr Mackintosh's three daughters were united in wedlock to their respective bridegrooms with one ceremony. Among the hundred guests who witnessed the rite on the green in front of the house, there was none who had ever been present at a like occurrence. Each of the brides wore a handsome dress of the same material with a white veil hanging down the back. The triple pair, along which the best men and brides' maids presented a most interesting appearance. The combined marriage cake was beautifully ornamented in three large sections while the dinner in the barn was sumptuous and well cooked.

(25th) Some weeks ago a strange bird was observed to have taken up a temporary abode in a wood near Glenferness House. Naturally it became an object of great curiousity in the locality and in consequence had the misfortune to fall victim to the gun of a tenant farmer. It was then sent to the Schoolhouse for identification, and was found to be a fine specimen of the Great Cinereous Shrike *Lanius excubitor*, a very rare visitor on our side of the Grampians. It also gets the name of Butcher Bird, from its peculiar habit of impaling its prey on some sharp thorn in hedge or bush before devouring it. So far as we know, the only other appearances in the district are, one in the year 1836, another ten years later, and a third in 1889.

May (19th) I was delighted this afternoon to receive J.A. Harvie-Brown, Esquire of Dunipace, who drove up from Forres to see my husband's collection. He is the joint editor of 'The Annals of Scottish Natural History'. He is a great authority on the British Fauna and is said to possess the finest private natural history library and museum in Scotland. He was greatly interested in our specimens and said that

Great Grey Shrike

their chief value lay in that they were obtained within a definite area, being practically representative of Nairnshire . . .

Ferness School Log Book: *May – 'The school is immensely improved in comfort and appearance by the substitution of clear glass for that previously used in the windows'.*

June (13th) This afternoon Sir William Cameron Gull gave an excellent political address – my husband in the chair – to the Glenferness electors, and he afterwards came in to the Schoolhouse and had tea from me. His father was the eminent physician who detected the wasting of the thyroid gland in females, causing great swelling over the system and known as Myxoedema. For his treatment of the Prince of Wales in 1871 he received a baronetcy. (15th) Miss Clunas, Nairn, having returned from Gibraltar where she was spending a holiday, has presented us with a number of curious grasses which she collected on the Rock. They form a most interesting addition to our Herbarium . . .

(24th) For several days past a trustful mousie, to the delight of the scholars, has been coming boldly out from its retreat in the school wall and takes great liberty in searching for crumbs over the floor. From its sleek and plump appearance we conclude that it must rank as one of the 'upper ten' of its own social community. It compares very favourably with those unfortunate members whose lot it is to live a life of penury among empty pews and in consequence gave rise to the saying – 'As poor as a church mouse'. (28th) Some time ago Mr William Clunas suggested and designed a Cabinet for Robert's natural history specimens, and to-day the finished article has been sent for up from Nairn. As the cabinet-maker complains that he has made no profit on it we are to give him £11.15.0 or thirty shillings over the contract price, and the Clunas family very generously pay one half of the whole cost, a kindness which we appreciate very highly indeed.

July (13th) Yesterday the Parliamentary Election for Elgin and Nairn took place and we are very sorry to learn that Sir William Cameron Gull has been defeated by a Mr Seymour Keay, who had a majority of 545. I expect that he will turn out a poor representative for the united counties in the House of Commons. Mr Robert Finlay has also lost his seat as member for the Inverness Burghs, by 53 votes in favour of a Mr Gilbert Beith who is an exceptionally weak man. Both men were returned as the result of their extravagant promises which can never be fulfilled by a Liberal Government. (29th) As Robert had to read a Paper to the Northern Scientific Societies in the Inverness Town Hall on the Rarer Flora of Ardclach and exhibit a number of plants, we both left Ferness at an early hour in order to have everything arranged in the room before the members met. Provost Ross was in the Chair and we were delighted to again meet Mr and Mrs Horne of the Geological Survey; Mr Wallace, Rector of the High

School; Mr James Fraser, C.E., and Dr Aitken, the Medical Superintendent of the Lunatic Asylum. Everyone appeared to be greatly interested in our local Botany and acknowledged the valuable service which my husband had rendered to the objects of the Societies in collecting and classifying the subalpine Flora of Nairnshire. Although it was four o'clock next morning before we reached Ferness, we were very much pleased with our every experience. During the week I have received several presents – blackcurrants, strawberries and cream, together with new potatoes, and a beautiful Shetland shawl. Surely I ought to be grateful for my many mercies.

October (7th) Regret to observe in the newspaper that Lord Tennyson of Aldworth, the poet-laureate, died yesterday at his country seat. I hope he will be buried in Westminster Abbey. His lovely lyrics are all written with great care and will, no doubt, continue to be a source of great intellectual enjoyment to readers of verse for generations yet to come.

November (8th) This season there was really no harvest in Ardclach till the month of October and even then the weather proved very unfavourable both for reaping and ingathering. Much damage has been caused by wind and rain, with not a little snow and occasionally frost overnight, so that the yield must be considerably under an average. The rainfall for October as recorded at Glenferness House was 8.26 inches! (25th) By post Robert had a very interesting letter from the Rev Dr Gordon, Birnie, along with a present of a standard work on the British Fresh Water Molluscs. As these creatures live entirely in the liquid element and often among mud at the bottom of fairly deep pools, the charm of beauty and variety, so lavishly displayed in their shells is known only to the patiently industrious naturalist.

December

Ferness School Log Book: roads difficult.

(31st) In the evening we all went over to Achagour to our New Year's dinner. The roads were pleasantly hard with frost while the moon shone bright and soft in a cloudless sky. As usual the family were exceedingly kind and the conversation throughout was lively, instructive and high toned . . .

1893

January . . . (7th) Some three weeks ago a Snow Bunting *Plectrophenax nivalis*, in full plumage, from the far North was shot at Tomnarroch and handed over to my husband, who sent it for preservation to Inverness. It has now been returned beautifully set up and was today added to our collection. This pretty little bird of the

Finch family, though only a winter visitor to our country, often occurs about farm yards in large flocks during severe weather, and occasionally remains over the spring months to nest on the summits of the highest mountains in Sutherland and Shetland. (20th) Have been laid up for a few days with a rather severe attack of influenza. Not being able to attend schoool, my dear children never neglect before they are dismissed in the afternoon, to ask Robert if 'the Mistress is any better tonight?'. Several neighbours have also called at the house and Fortune, from her Horn of Plenty, has been filling our pantry with many unexpected gifts. In consequence my husband thinks that it pays better for me to be indisposed than at work, and suggests that I should be in no hurry leaving my sick room!

February (3rd) The annual concert in connection with the local Young Men's Association was held as usual in the school last night. The evening being fine, the house was crowded by a most enthusiastic and appreciative audience. Elsie and I had a good deal to do in giving tea in the class-room to some fifty people after the close, but the work and excitement quite cured me of a slight rheumatic affection which had been troubling me during the day.

Ferness School Log Book: 27 February – roads blocked.

March (10th) The Glenferness gamekeeper brought Robert four grouse eggs which had lain in the nest on the moor of Aitnoch since last spring. When blown, the albumen and yolk in each scarcely showed a trace of decomposition. The shells, which looked bright and clear, were found under the microscope to be poreless and hence the contents were hermetically sealed by Nature. They are now in our cabinet. This morning a poor horse belonging to Mr McAinsh, wood-merchant, fell over a steep rock on the Tomnarroch burn and was instantly killed.

(31st) A special meeting was held this evening in the schoolroom. The Young Men invited some thirty private friends to hear a Debate on the question – Should bachelors be taxed? The speakers on the affirmative side maintained that they should because, being interested in themselves alone, they were as a rule well off but failing to do their duty to the nation. Their opponents tried to show that the Bachelor

Snow Bunting

was a jolly good fellow contributing his due share to the national revenue and even contentedly paying his school rates for which he derived no immediate benefit. After the clock struck twelve, Robert sent several of the young folk into the class-room where we were preparing tea, to see if they could identify a beautiful handkerchief which I had got, and each one, when told it was the first of April laughed as they turned away somewhat disconcertedly at the roguish trick that had been played upon them! All however, went well, and every one seemed very happy.

April (10th) Yesterday a tramp was found dead at the riverside near Dunearn. The body was very lightly clad, and as death had taken place some eight or ten days previously, the burying beetles, *Silpha* and *Necrophori*, in great numbers, were busily engaged in their all important duty of breaking up the remains and restoring them to the dust whence they came. Poor fellow! He was some mother's son and perhaps, in early life, gave promise that he was to be a useful, or even an honoured member of society. But alas! his life did not prove a success, for his Plans, being ill-conceived, only went from bad to worse, till he had to beg his bread from door to door and, at last, yield his spirit on a lonely moor with no one to comfort him in his hour of weakness and need. His death was registered here by the local authorities, but without the usual particulars of his family connections.

(15th) After school I went to see a number of sick people on the Ferness side of the river and being overtaken by the minister got a drive in his machine. Although on the same errand, he did not visit so many families or stay so long as I would have done, had I been alone. On the way back a loud peal of thunder broke overhead and we were suddenly caught in a heavy shower of rain which drenched me to the skin. Soon however, the sun again came out and chased away the clouds, leaving the sky once more a rich dazzling blue. Our son Robert has taken rooms in Edinburgh for a few weeks and has asked his sister to come and join him for a short holiday.

May (3rd) This has been really a lovely day with at times a threatening of rain which would be welcome. The crops however, have made a good start, and look much better than they often do at this season of the year. The Mavis appears exceedingly happy, filling the evening air with its pretty refrain 'Cheer up, Cheer up', which may be considered the key-note of its song during the summer months. (17th) The School was examined by Mr Macleod, who was very pleasant and expressed himself quite satisfied with the results. He stayed and had dinner with us in the afternoon. The little Black-headed Gulls *Larus ridibundus*, or 'Pickie-tars' as they are locally called, are now nesting very freely in the marsh at the Loch of Belivat, and a neighbour sent me over four dozen of their eggs. For the table, they are usually hard-boiled, then shelled and eaten with a knife and fork. Thus prepared, most people consider them a great delicacy . . .

June (3rd) In the afternoon Robert went over to Achagour and stayed till past ten o'clock when he found that a dense mist had settled down. Desiring to get home withour delay, and being quite familiar with the Belivat moor, he hoped to shorten the journey by crossing it. In the fog however, he lost his bearings and, after a time, was greatly amazed to find that the sound of the gulls in the neighbouring loch was on the right instead of the left hand. After wandering aimlessly for over an hour he came out, strange to say, at the very spot where he went in. There was now no help for it but to walk round by the highway, past the post office and Logie Bridge . . . (20th) Today I got a basket of new potatoes from a neighbour. This is I think, the earliest date of which we ever before had a dish of locally grown ones. The *Solanum tuberosum* properly cooked and eaten with fresh herrings make a most luxurious meal in the cottage, and not less so even in the Royal Palace. The weather for some time past, has been rather cold, raw and unsettled. About mid-day however, a mild rain began to fall and will, no doubt, help greatly in stimulating the struggling crops.

(21st) In the afternoon twenty two of the Nairnshire teachers drove to the schoolhouse in three brakes and had tea with us on their homeward journey from a picnic at Lynemore. We were glad to meet with so many of the brethren and pleased to hear that they had enjoyed their excursion among our upland wilds. This was, no doubt, due in great measure to the lovely vegetation at this season, as well as the beautiful scenery at Dulsie Bridge and the Rock Walk, which many of them saw for the first time in their short walk along our section of the Findhorn. Scarcely less interesting to a few with antiquarian tastes, was the mysterious Princess Stone on whose

The Princess Stone (both sides)

strange symbols the grey lichen has reflected the evening sunsets of more than a thousand years.

July . . . (6th) This being the marriage day of their Royal Highnesses the Duke of York and the Princess Mary of Teck, we gave a tea to all our scholars after they had finished lessons in the evening, and Mrs MacKenzie of the shop, having come in to help us, handed each child a large parcel of confection at the close. Seeing that the August pair, as heirs presumptive, may sit one day on the Throne, I hope the union now consummated may prove an unqualified blessing in every respect. From all we hear, the lady is likely to prove a 'crown of rejoicing' both to her husband and the British nation, if spared, in due time, to become the Queen Consort. (15th) The Young Men having arranged to hold their annual picnic this year at Cawdor Castle, Robert and I were prevailed on, at the last moment, to join the party. As the morning was clear and pleasant with a dappled sky overhead, there seemed every indication that the weather would continue fine. I am now glad that we consented to go as our route led us past several well-remembered homesteads which brought to our recollection many happy experiences within their walls in bygone days. But alas! several of the kindly faces that used to smile on us were no more to be seen . . . We were grateful however, to meet not a few former friends. It was very refreshing to again hold sweet converse with them though it was rather depressing to observe the evidence of passing years in the silver hairs and wrinkled brows of those who were considered in the prime of their days when we were in the Parish.

The Young Men were greatly delighted with their visit to the Hermitage in the Achniem Burn. This remarkable stream is one of the most interesting pieces of sylvan scenery in the county. A natural rampart of conglomerate rock rises almost perpendicular on each side for more than a hundred feet above where the water gurgles below. These rugged cliffs are richly clothed with clumps of native wood; pine, birch and hazel as well as a profusion of bush, and wild flower, which wave over crag and cranny all along its course from the uplands to the lower reaches. At the entrance to this singular ravine of exquisite beauty stands the historic Castle, amid some oak and ash trees that wrested admiration from Dr Johnson himself on his memorable visit in 1773. The Thane who laid the foundation about the year 1400 is said by local tradition, to have consulted a grey-haired seer as to the site. He was told to put a coffer containing the necessary gold on the back of an ass and erect his Peel with the money, at the third hawthorn tree at which the gnostic creature should stop. This advice was followed and the grim Tower was built round the precious stem which we all saw in the Dungeon Keep.

About a hundred years later a large wing was added. In the drawing room there is a carved stone chimney-piece dated 1510, with several grotesque figures. Among them are a cat playing a fiddle, a monkey blowing a horn and curiously enough, a fox smoking a tobacco pipe, some seventy years before the introduction of the 'divine weed'. It also bears a Latin inscription – *Ceri mani memoneris mane*: Remember in the morning the good Creator; or as a waggish bishop rendered it – Remain long at night, and remember it in the morning. The walls of the more modern apartments are not plastered but hung with tapestry, and the antique high-backed chairs and curious old mirrors still remain. In one of the rooms a bed used to be shown wherein 'the gracious King Duncan' was said to have been murdered by Macbeth, but in 1815 a fire broke out in the division of the Castle, and so the Royal couch was destroyed. On the way home a very heavy shower came on, but it had no effect in damping the enthusiasm of our friends who were all delighted with the day's experiences.

(29th) Today Elsie has been a successful exhibitor at the Auldearn and Ardclach Industrial Show, having got four first prizes for a Rag Rug, a knitted Bed cover, a pair of Socks, and Flour Scones, but only second for a Seed Cake which she expected would carry all before it. (31st) Mr George Bain of the 'Nairnshire Telegraph' sent Robert a copy of his new 'History of Nairnshire' with the Author's Compliments. It is a large volume of very great and permanent value, bearing testimony to a careful survey of the field which it has been elected to cover. We greatly appreciate the Work as it gives, with remarkable lucidity, a lengthened and unusually interesting account of many places, scenes and legends in the county with which we are both familiar.

August (30th) A beautiful butterfly, *Vanessa atlanta* [Red Admiral], not very often seen so far north, has made its appearance in considerable numbers along the Findhorn valley. The great heat of the past summer has no doubt been favourable to its complete development both in the caterpillar and chrysalis stages. The female hibernates through the winter, then after laying her eggs on the small nettle, *Urtica urens*, she usually seeks a sheltered cranny in some decaying tree or other suitable retreat, and calmly resigns herself to the fate of all living. (31st) Sorry to hear that poor John Alexander, an old acquaintance on the Meikle Burn, has rashly taken his departure from this life, and today his friends and neighbours interred all that death had left in the Parish churchyard by the riverside. His arithmetical bump was abnormally developed and in consequence he could work mentally, and without effort, astonishingly large sums, such as multiplying £578–16–9 by 657; or run up simultaneously three columns of a simple or compound addition question seven or eight lines high and invariably give the correct answer in so short a time that, to the ordinary mind, the feat was truly amazing.

When trudging along on his daily routine as the Nairn and Cawdor postrunner, he often amused himself by conning over such a problem as, If a square foot contain so many stalks of oats, each bearing a given average of seeds on its panicle, How many grains should the farmer ingather from a field of say, ten or twenty acres? John, though often asked, was quite unable to make any intelligible explanation of the process by which he arrived at his results. He remained in the service of the Post Office for several years, was very obliging, and much liked as a public servant.

October (2nd) We opened school today and got the various classes so fairly arranged that we expect the work to go on smoothly for some time to come. In the evening I visited several families and found in each, one or two members, owing to the changeable weather of the past few days, complaining of coughs or colds, but all were able to converse so cheerfully that I think the worst is over. Elsie got her prize money by post for her exhibits at the Auldearn Show. Rachel Sinton looked in for a few minutes and gave me a basket of plums and a bunch of grapes.

November (25th) Lady Leven called here today and in the evening held the first meeting of her proposed Scottish Mothers' Union in our schoolroom. There was a full attendance but more, I suspect, on account of her Ladyship's personal invitation than from any real interest in the movement. A few were confirmed old maids, several were matrons whose families had all grown up and even left the parish, while the remainder were active mothers with their children still under the parental roof, and all the better for wise and seasonable advice. After a good tea the Rev David Miller gave an admirable address on the duties, trials, and pleasures connected with the spiritual and temporal upbringing of the young. Some of the goodwives called previously at the schoolhouse and gave me a fowl, eggs, butter and cream. In a letter we had from Elsie we are glad to learn that our son has got an increase of salary from his chief Dr McGowan, and that arrangements are being made by which Robert is to leave Bellshill at an early date, and set up practice on his own account in Uddingston.

December (16th) We are very sorry to learn by this morning's 'Courier' that the Rev George Gordon, L.L.D., parish minister of Birnie, near Elgin has departed this life, and entered upon his eternal rest. As an ardent lover of Nature he was an esteemed friend and correspondent of my husband for many years. In the fields of Geology, Botany, and Entomology he was a leading authority and easily took a prominent place in the front rank among his like-minded brethren in the north of Scotland. While exploring the local Old Red Sandstone deposits, he was fortunate enough to discover a new fossil reptile which, in recognition of his great ability was named *Hyperodapedon Gordoni*. On many occasions his counsels and guidance were eagerly sought, and as readily given, to amateurs who cared to show a genuine interest in any scientific pursuit, within the Old Province of Moray.

The other week Ex-Bailie Stewart of Inverness gave a most interesting lecture on Canada to a crowded audience in our school. During the two nights he stayed with us, we enjoyed his company exceedingly. Though generally quiet and unassuming, he was found, when occasion required, to be active and brim full of sparkling humour. In politics he was an advanced liberal, but seasoned his radical principles, we thought, with more common sense than is generally the case with many belonging to his party. From several literary pieces which he recited in the evening for our amusement, we saw that he was a fluent speaker and a wonderful mimic of rural peasant character . . .

1894

January (1st) To inaugurate another year I visited a few invalids on our side of the river Findhorn. From each I received a kindly welcome and enjoyed our social intercourse during the short time at my disposal. In one house the frail grandmother told me that she had now seen eighty winters but that the present one had been the hardest in her experience. There were days in which her family believed she would not see the evening and nights when it seemed to them that morning could only dawn for her in a fairer world. Again however, the unexpected had happened, and I found her wonderfully well. She was pleased to receive our good wishes for a 'happy new year' . . . (27th) The female teacher at Dulsie, having turned suddenly ill, is unable for duty and Elsie has been asked by the clerk of the School Board to take her place for a few days . . .

February (23rd) A neighbouring field labourer has been off work, and confined to bed for several weeks past. It was arranged by a few sympathizers, as he has ten dependents at his fireside, to hold a local concert to afford them some needed help in their present trouble and anxiety. Accordingly a large audience assembled in our schoolroom but as his own minister failed at the last moment to turn up Robert had to take the chair. The result however, was that the committee found itself in a position to hand over to the respected head of the house a little over £13. A friend who has just returned from Shetland presented Robert with four eggs of the Arctic Skua *Stercorarius crepidatus*, and another, who is newly home from Johannesburg, gave him two pieces of quartz freely impregnated with tiny gold nuggets yielding, we were told, from twenty to thirty ounces per ton of the precious metal. They have all been added to our collection.

May (14th) This was the day of our Government examination. Mr Macleod was here by eleven o'clock and brought two ladies with him to enjoy the beauties of the Findhorn near the schoolhouse. The children did remarkably well, especially in the lower standards. Although we never had the least reason to fear the visit of any inspector, we both invariably feel somewhat nervous for a few days previous to his arrival – and always experience a happy sense of relief when all is again over for another year. Robert gave the scholars a well-deserved holiday which will enable me to complete a few household arrangements left over in connection with my recent spring cleaning . . .

Ferness School Log Book: 32 boys and 13 girls present. Inspector's comment – A new map of Scotland is required and a gate should be placed across the entrance to the school to prevent outsiders getting admission to the playground.

June . . . (8th) Tonight we were glad to have Mr David Fraser, Belivat, a former pupil, and his wife, from the United States, at tea. He has done well in the land of his adoption and is an honour to his native parish. Our favourite cat 'Don' is every day bringing home one or more fairly sized rabbits which he proudly lays down on the floor and appears to seek praise for his clever and generous deeds. In the evening I went to see my sick neighbours, and was pleased to find that they were each much better and quite cheerful. (30th) About ten o'clock several members of the Nairn Literary Institute arrived at the schoolhouse in four brakes, and took my husband and Elsie to Carn Glass, a mountain which attains an elevation of 2162 feet on the southern boundary of the county. Near the summit, the Cloud-berry *Rubus chamaemorus*, was sparingly found among the sphagnum. It is a humble single-flowered growth with the true stem creeping underground. The fruit is an agglomeration of one-seeded juicy drupes which are usually ripe about the end of August. It has a very agreeable flavour and, when found in sufficient quantities, is often made into an excellent preserve.

The view all round, from the lofty Grampians fringing the southern sky to the far distant Ord of Caithness on the north, was most impressive – a rare panorama which the ordinary individual can only seldom expect to see even during a long lifetime. Before descending to the plain below, the party recorded its visit with the names of all present on a sheet of paper and, putting the document in a champagne bottle, securely built it up in the bottom of the ordnance cairn which marks the highest point on the summit. As few travellers pass this way it would be interesting to speculate as to the time and circumstances when it will be discovered.

July, . . . *Ferness School Log Book: (6th) 'great heat, low attendance'* (28th) While our son was here for a few days, two other friends

Robert and Elsie Thomson, probably on their marriage.
Photo: Mrs H. Lamb

Todlochy, Aberdeenshire, today.
Photo: J. Love.

Cawdor Castle.
Photo: J. Love.

Ardclach Church and churchyard earlier this century. The foot-bridge over the Findhorn to Ferness was washed away in 1958. *Photo: Mr & Mrs F. Masson.*

Ardclach churchyard, in a hollow beside the wooded banks of the River Findhorn. *Photo: J. Love.*

Ardclach Schoolhouse—no longer occupied.
Photo: J. Love.

Ardclach Bell Tower.
Photo: J. Love.

Ferness School as it was in 1900.
Photo: Mr & Mrs J. MacBean.

Ferness as it is today. The schoolhouse (now much altered) is on the right. *Photo: J. Love.*

The Ferness blacksmith at work.
Photo: Mrs & Mrs F. Masson

The mail arriving from Dunphail at Glenferness Post Office.
The local postman stands on the left,
and the Schoolhouse is in the background.
Photo: Mr & Mrs W. Macleod

Donald MacQueen, the carpenter, at his workshop near Dulsie Bridge in 1884. *Photo: Mr E. Brodie of Lethen.*

Miss Murdoch with the children of Knockandu School (now the keeper's house) near Dulsie Bridge in 1884. *Photo: Mr E. Brodie of Lethen.*

Dulsie Bridge over the River Findhorn.
Photo: J. Love.

from the south called and I had four Roberts at dinner. During the last fortnight not a few of my neighbours have looked in to see me, and have stocked my pantry with grapes, butter, eggs and new potatoes, as well as rabbits, jam and bottles of cream. Surely 'Goodness and Mercy have followed me' and we should now cease to entertain groundless anxieties for the future.

August (8th) Through the greater part of the by-gone week the weather has been rather disappointing, being showery along with occasional peals of distant thunder. There were intervals of bright sunshine, though each day was more or less cloudy with a keen cold temperature at night. Gradually however, the sky became completely overcast, and from early morn till late in the evening on Saturday a heavy rain fell making outdoor movement very disagreeable. A poor Rook was shot today in a field near Ferness and, as there were quite a few white feathers in the wings, it was sent to Robert as a curiosity. (10th) This is my dear husband's birthday. The mutual sympathy which brought us together in Cawdor many years ago, has grown steadily stronger and deeper up to the present times . . . (31st) Dr Mackie of Elgin who examined Robert's natural history collection a few weeks ago, has just paid him a very kindly tribute in the 'Elgin Courant'.

'The Schoolmaster as a Man of Science' – read by Dr Mackie, Elgin before the Morayshire Educational Institute: –

Only a few months ago I had the pleasure of looking over the collection of Mr Robert Thomson, Schoolmaster of Ardclach. He has been known to the scientific world for many years as an enthusiastic botanist and entomologist. His herbarium contains considerably over four hundred flowering plants and ferns, or quite a third of the total flora of Scotland – all collected from the parish of Ardclach or its immediate precincts. This is a more extensive flora than one would naturally expect from such a limited area, but the rocky and romantic gorge of the Findhorn, with numerous sylvan dales at intervals, the side-reaches of natural and cultivated woodland that border it on either side, the heathery moor of Aitnoch and the broom clad wastes around the Loch of Belivat, all combined to make the Ardclach district a happy hunting ground for both botanist and entomologist. Mr Thomson has availed himself of the advantages of this unique position to the full . . . [He] has also studied the Mosses and believes that his local list of the species is now nearly complete. At one period of his life he also devoted some attention to geology, and discovered one or more outliers of the basal Conglomerates of the Old Red in Ardclach . . . In Entomology, Mr Thomson has also added much to our knowledge of not a few of the rarer moths and butterflies, several of his captures being first records for these species north of the Grampians . . . Here is a curious beetle that may interest you. The same gentleman has been found by Mr Thomson in the woods of

Ardclach. He goes by the name of the Highland Timberman. His peculiarity is the extreme length of the feelers, which sometimes reach to nearly four inches. How he manages to fly through the tangled thickets of Ardclach without taking these long moustacheos out of twist is more than Mr Thomson, or any other naturalist has yet been able to tell us.

The bird fauna of Ardclach is also very varied and Mr Thomson has been able to collect the eggs of about eighty different species. Among them are four specimens laid by some hapless Jackdaw in probably her third attempt to hatch a brood of gorblings in the ruined wall of Lochindorbh Castle, but as her colouring matter had become quite exhausted, the clutch in question was almost perfectly white. Then there is an egg of that curious bird the Goat-sucker [Nightjar], which though not quite so rare as that of the Great Auk is, in Mr Thomson's opinion, perhaps the most interesting specimen in his collection. After hatching her young one the parent hen seems to have removed the broken shell in two complete sections only a few feet from the nest. These parts Mr Thomson gummed and pieced together so neatly that one would scarcely know that this egg could ever have been broken, so as to release in due course, a living chick. In addition to local birds, he notes as occasional visitors the Goldfinch, the Crossbill, the Great grey shrike and, in winter the Snow Bunting.

Not the least interesting fact I have to record regarding the Naturalist of Ardclach is that he has several enthusiastic helpers in his work. In a list of the Butterflies and Moths of Ardclach, published early last year in the Annals of Scottish Natural History, I find Mrs Thomson is credited with the capture of a few of the rarer species, while the names 'Willie Scott, Jamie Anderson' and one or two others, evidently pupils, stand opposite several of the rarest in the list. Inspiration has been going on here. There is no greater incentive to a boy's enthusiasm than the knowledge that he may take part in the legitimate pursuits of men, and it is always a healthy sign to see teacher and pupil with common interests in things outside the immediate pale of school work.

September (4th) This is the anniversary of our marriage thirty two years ago. Of the sixty friends who sat down to dinner in the Meikle Geddes granary after the ceremony, the great majority has passed through the vale of oblivion to their eternal rest, and I could easily

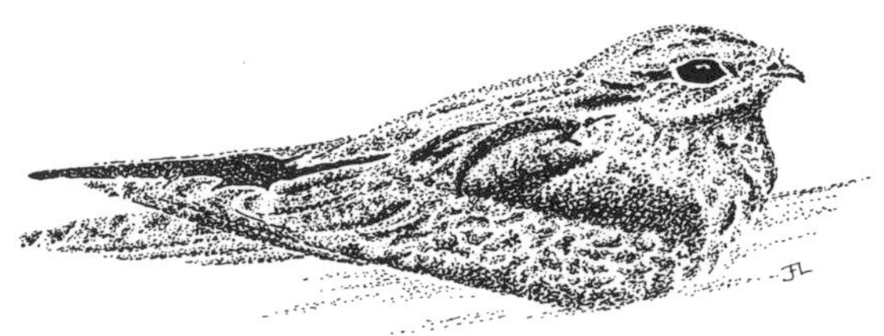

Nightjar

count on my fingers those who yet remain in the land of the living. To ourselves the union has proved an unmixed blessing . . .

October (1st) We opened the school today with a fair number of scholars. At noon there came from Robert a letter in which he speaks of going into a new house at Uddingston. (8th) This was a beautiful day and all the farmers round are very busy taking in their oats to the stack-yard. The village children were enjoying themselves to the full on the harvest field nearby when a rather serious accident occurred. While Charlie Mackenzie was hanging in play on the hind part of a loaded cart, he allowed his head to get in between the iron stanchion which supports the side of the box and the moving wheel, with the result that the scalp was cut and largely peeled off from his skull. Robert and I were called in and carefully washed the wound. When Dr Mann came he had little to do beyond putting in five stitches. I hope this may be a warning to the wee boy and a lesson to the others, not to be often thoughtless in running foolhardy risks.

November

Ferness School Log Book: (16th) James Muirhead and Grace Innes each had feet scalded by hot water at home.

(23rd) Dr Macaulay, one of our son's fellow students, when on a voyage to India as ship's surgeon, managed to procure a pair of Ostrich eggs at Aden, and sent them to my husband for our collection. During the hatching season the female bird scoops out a very simple nest in the sand and usually lays from eight to ten yellowish-white eggs, each weighing about three pounds. In removing one or more from the clutch, the native always uses a long stick bent at the end, in order that the hen may not take alarm at the human touch and in consequence, abandon her treasures . . .

(28th) A very fine specimen of a beautifully marked moth was sent over here from Glenferness House for identification and proved to be *Polia chi* [Grey Chi], a distinctly local insect in general, though fairly frequent in our parish. Nature in her sportive mood has impressed the Greek letter X near the centre of each upper wing and hence the name of the species. Nor is this all. She has portrayed with mystic hand, at least four more characters from the Hellenic alphabet on a few others, for example, the Gray Dagger *Acronycta psi*, *Plusia iota* [Golden], and *Plusia gamma* [Silver], but what is perhaps more wonderful still she has registered on the wings of *Argynnis aglaia*, and *A. selene*, Arabic markings which many have read as crudely formed figures corresponding with important dates in the Christian era.

December (4th) Mrs Mackenzie, Post Office, gave my husband a very fine pocket handkerchief for his attention in dressing her poor Charlie's head. The wound is not quite healed – a result which I did not expect to see at the time it occurred. Today one of our scholars, Andrew Mackenzie, in climbing about the Ferness carrier's cart, which was left for a short time standing up on its spurs at the roadside near the school, fell and broke the tibia bone of his right leg. Robert and I set it very gently and supported the fracture with strips of strong cardboard. He was sent home to Keppernach as comfortably as possible, from where his father went off with him to the hospital at Nairn. There the house surgeon completed the dressing. During his stay as an inmate the little fellow became a great favourite with every one in the institution and when discharged, was very sorry parting with his kind nurses. In bidding them goodbye he expressed a wish that he might soon have another broken limb so as to be in a position to return!

Ferness School Log Book: Andrew Mackenzie's unfortunate accident is the only one of any consequence within school hours in 38 years.

1895

Ferness School Log Book: January and February: roads often blocked and little school. February (22nd) Water pipe in the classroom burst and flooded both rooms.

March (27th) Mr James Mackillican, Calcutta, being in want of a good man for one of his tea gardens near Darjeeling, Robert recommended an old pupil Mr John Macdonald, the Meikle Lyne. This evening they have both gone over to Achagour to hear the terms. After some consideration Mr John has accepted and we are sure that each party has made an excellent bargain.

April (6th) After visiting a sick neighbour I had, on returning home, to go to bed with a severe attack of bile. Several of my village friends called in the evening to ask for me. We were pleased to hear from his mother that our old scholar Alexander Macpherson, Glenferness, has got a good situation in the forest of the Duke of Rutland at Belvoir Castle in Leicestershire and is going south in a few days . . . (22nd) Tonight a deputation consisting of Messrs Peter Innes, James Rose, Ludovic Alexander, William Macglashan and Robert, went over to the Meikle Lyne with the Testimonial to be presented to Mr John Macdonald on the eve of his departure for India. In handing him a very handsome Gladstone bag along with a purse of sovereigns, my husband told him that many young men and women had gone out from our little county of Nairnshire, and distinguished themselves in all parts of the world 'from Greenland's icy mountains to India's coral strand'. As the list contained not a few from the parish of Ardclach his friends would specially watch his future career with the utmost confidence, that in due time, the honourable roll would be extended by the addition of another name dear to them all . . .

(23rd) A note came from Logie Bridge stating that our dear old neighbour, Janet Macbean, 'Auntie', was passing away. Dressing quickly, I hurried over, but failed to reach before she had joined the majority. Her sister told me that the end was very pleasant and that she left her blessing to us all, mentioning each by name. To me as well as to many others, she was a true friend, living a devout and useful life in her own sphere. As a genuine Christian she will be long remembered with affection and admiration . . .

May (8th) Mrs Ogston, the wife of the Marischal College Professor, with a lady friend from Aberdeen came to the schoolhouse and stayed with us for two days. They were touring the country north of the Grampians by easy stages in their private phaeton and wished particularly to have a look at the scenery on the Findhorn. The parish church from the Ferness bank impressed them as singularly grand and picturesque. Not less were they delighted with their visit to the Rock Walk and Dulsie Bridge, where at both places the river has cut for itself a narrow passage between massive ramparts shaded to the water's edge with pine, birch and hazel. Seldom if ever, they told us, had they seen finer 'bits' on any other river. We greatly enjoyed their society and felt very sorry when they left.

(14th) This was our examination day. Although dull at sunrise, the morning was dry and pleasant with a light breeze just sufficient to bend the tops of the tall trees. During the forenoon the clouds rolled away and the day turned out all that could be desired. Punctually at the hour appointed the Inspector drove up in a carriage and pair, having with him three ladies who spent some time, while we were on duty, along the river bank and returned in due course to join us at dinner. Like our other friends, they were loud in praise of the lovely scenery through which the stream rushes on its way to the sea. The children did very well in each class, notwithstanding the great irregularity in the attendance during the past year.

Ferness School Log Book: The mantlepiece is tumbling down, and one

Redstart

of the lattice windows of the lobby fell in by a gust of wind on the day of inspection.

(17th) Today we got by post a handsome copy of 'Sir Victor Brooke, Sportsman and Naturalist' from Mrs Ogston as well as her husband's photograph of which I am very proud. (30th) Our school Report has now come and is very gratifying to both Robert and myself. In the evening three farmers' wives called at the schoolhouse and brought me butter, eggs and cream. Rain has been falling since yesterday but the amount is so small that I am afraid it will not be of much benefit to the struggling crops.

June (5th) A pair of Redstarts *Ruticilla phoenicurus*, on their arrival from the south about a fortnight ago, began to repair their last year's nest in the farmer's letter-box on the roadside at Airdrie, near here. I trust that nothing untoward may happen to the interesting couple, as this is the fourth season in which they have successively returned to hatch and rear their young in a very exceptional kind of domicile. The nest is rather loosely constructed of moss and dry grass, with a lining of hair and feathers in an empty corner, and the happy mother sits on her light blue eggs quite indifferent to the postman's daily consignment of letters and newspapers. The male, as if proud to show off his beautiful plumage, may generally be seen restlessly flitting from one low branch to another, or perched on some elevated ridge or weather-beaten stone not far away, complacently uttering his faint but musical song to cheer and encourage his beloved mate in her lonely hours.

(22nd) This morning Elsie and her father joined the Young Men's Association in their picnic to Lochindorbh. Owing to the high wind they did not risk sailing over to the Castle, but had lunch on the shore at the nearest point. Before leaving, Robert read a paper on the grim old stronghold. It was he said, an object of the greatest interest to the antiquary. There were no records to show when or by whom it was erected, but Tradition told of a rude crannog having originally

Lochindorbh Castle

occupied the site, although no remains had been found . . . The Castle comes into view about the year 1230, when a Comyn, Lord of Badenoch was frequently found taking up his abode in this all but invincible pile.

Robert the Second ascended the throne in 1371 and among his first acts we find him conferring the Forest and Castle of Lochindorbh upon his fourth son Alexander Stewart, the Lord of Badenoch. From the savageness of his nature he is better known in the north as the Wolfe. In his domestic capacity this nobleman was unprincipled, heartless and cruel. He so ill-treated his wife, the Countess of Ross, that she was forced to leave him. During her absence he became enamoured of a woman named Mariota Athyn, by whom he had five illegitimate sons, each of whom inherited the lawless violence of his father. At last the Church was invoked to interfere on behalf of his lawful wife – a proceeding which exasperated the Wolfe in a terrible degree. Disregarding all right of property he seized the Church lands and was excommunicated at the high Altar by the Bishop of Moray. Furious with rage the Wolfe matured his plans and, sallying out from his stronghold in May 1390, set fire to Forres. Still burning with rage he determined to beard the lion in his den, and in one night the towers and spires of Elgin Cathedral were wrapt in a brilliant sheet of dazzling flame.

Exalting in the hope that the interference on the part of the Bishop had been fully avenged, he shut himself up within his surly keep, only to find that the dull monotony simply served to quicken the qualms of conscience. Thus tortured, he sunk into a state of profound melancholy, and in a few weeks was completely prostrated – the victim of a low consuming fewer . . . By and by the climax was reached, and with it a great improvement in his natural character. Soon after the Wolfe was induced by penance to be again received within the pale of the Holy Mother Church. To this the Bishop agreed, and the strange humiliation took place in the Black Friars' Monastery at Perth before the highest dignitaries both in the Church and State . . . In 1455 James the Second granted a commission to William, Thane of Cawdor, to raze and destroy the Fortalice of Lochindorbh and, when this work was duly accomplished, the noble Baron left the ancient keep very much as we see it.

A local tradition asserts that the massive iron door now in the dungeon of Cawdor Castle was carried at least the distance of thirteen miles across the moor on the shoulders of a powerful Highlander known in his day as 'Donal gun mhaithair', or Donald without a mother.

I, and our son, who was with us for a few days, drove up [to Lochindorbh] in the afternoon. By that time the gale had subsided and everything again looked fresh and pleasant. On our arrival we stabled the pony at the home of an old scholar, and were pressed by his mother to wait and have tea. At the hour appointed she had on a spotless table, loaf, homemade bannocks and cake, with biscuit, butter and jam. A jug of rich cream together with a basin of fresh eggs stood in the centre. Of the latter we each had a couple set before us and were even offered a third. As the mountain air had quickened our appetite, we enjoyed our meal to the full. Speaking of the Castle, which we saw from the window, our hostess remarked that she herself had only been once over at the ruin but, as no boat was available at the time, 'How,' she asked, 'did I get across?' When we had each made one or two futile guesses she laughingly said, 'On the ice of course.' Soon after our whole Party, whom circumstances had gathered for the first, and probably the last time, again scattered, but our social intercourse left many pleasant effects on all our minds.

September (28th) On the invitation of Dr Mackie, one of the Directors of the Elgin Museum, we spent a couple of days in town while Robert was engaged in re-arranging and naming the local collection of birds' eggs in the various cases.

Having a few hours to spare at the end, we both visited the ruins of the famous cathedral on the left bank of the river Lossie. This once glorious edifice was a cruciform purely Gothic structure with two western towers and a splendid central spire. The grand doorway, windows and Pillars are adorned with foliage, grapes and other carvings. On the north side stands the Chapter House in which we saw the beautiful 'Prentice Pillar' whose singular engravings and traceries are scarcely surpassed by those on a similar column at Roslin. . . (30th) For a few hours this morning Robert was very ill. When getting out of bed he suddenly fell on the floor in a faint, owing to a sharp darting pain in the left side. As there was no fever it seemed to be caused by a kind of neuralgia among the intercostal muscles. In a short time however, he was dripping all over with a profuse perspiration and we both thought that death was near at hand. It was not yet to be and I thank God that, by the afternoon, my dear husband was quite restored to his usual condition.

October

Ferness School Log Book: 2nd – One and a half inches of rain fell in 18 hours.

Slow worm

(3rd) The other day a pretty large reptile was caught at Dulsie Bridge and sent down to Robert as a terrible *serpens horridus*. The captor felt specially proud that he had been able to force it, without serious consequences, into an ordinary quart bottle which was thereafter firmly corked and so made absolutely safe for the bearer. At a glance, it was found to be neither a serpent, nor even a viper, but simply a very fine specimen of the Blind or Slow-worm *Anguis fragilis*, one of the most harmless of creeping things with no more power to inflict an injury than the common earth-worm. Should it happen to be rather roughly seized it often resorts to a curious trick of snapping off its tail in its captor's hands, and if possible dropping to the ground and slipping quietly away among the thick foliage. True to its nocturnal nature it comes out chiefly under cover of darkness and eats up large numbers of snails, slugs, and grubs, thus proving an excellent friend to the farmer as well as the gardener. Owing however to a general ignorance of its life history, combined with a very serpent-like appearance, it often suffers death most undeservedly as the result of leaving a safe retreat and showing itself during the day.

(6th) Yesterday, Robert received for the Nairn Museum a box with a few Natural History specimens picked up by Captain Wallace when abroad. One of these was the curious creature known as the Sea Horse *Hippocampus brevirostis*. When swimming, it maintains a vertical position but the tail which entwines in any direction is ready to grasp whatever suitable object it may meet in the water and, when securely fixed, darts the head at its prey with great dexterity. This tiny sea-monster which derives its name from the remarkable likeness of the head and neck to those of the horse, appears as if clad in a kind of rough armour, which bristles with numerous prominent tubercles, or even spines, all over the body. It is supposed to have been the original of the fiery spirited steed with golden mane and brazen hoofs, so often represented as drawing, with great swiftness, the elegant shell-chariot of Neptune over the dancing waves.

November (27th) When it became known a few weeks ago that Mr Ludovic Alexander, our postrunner between Ferness and Dunphail, was to be put on the retired list, a general feeling was at once expressed along his route, that he should receive some tangible token of goodwill and respect. Accordingly in a short time, a handsome sum of money was placed in the hands of the committee and my husband, along with a deputation of local gentlemen were appointed to wait upon him yesterday at Logie Bridge. On their arrival Robert stated the object of their visit, and thereafter called upon Mr John Mann, farmer, Cairnglass to make the presentation to Mr Alexander of a handsome marble timepiece and a purse of sovereigns, together with a silver tea service, and cake-basket to his wife.

1896

Ferness School Log Book: January 10th – Inspector's report: – The scheme of Elementary Science for this school has been approved by the Department, though recommending it should be more experimental and observational.

February

Ferness School Log Book: 7th – ex-Ballie Stuart lectured on the Dominion of Canada here last night.

(22nd) The other day we received from Alexander Mann, Esq. of Guayaquil, Ecuador, a small box containing the skins of a dozen humming birds, the naked bodies of which could not have much exceeded in size those of our common bumblebee. When alive they must have been charming little creatures, as the most superb hues of even the costliest gems fade before the glittering brilliancy of the young cavalier when he shines out, after his second year, in all the radiance of his nuptial array. Such beauty was surely intended to please mankind, but more especially I think, to delight the keen eyes of these bright beings themselves. The females generally speaking, are without the splendour of the males, as they are clad in modest, not to say even plain and sombre plumage.

The nest which has never more than two eggs, is a wonderful structure. It is composed of the softest materials with a view to warmth, and covered by suitable lichens, which are never turned the wrong way. These birds are very bold in defence of their young and do not hesitate to attack, with their needle-like bills, the eyes of even birds of prey which they far surpass in the extreme rapidity with which they dart through the air. Fitted exclusively for their own peculiar environment, almost every attempt to take a few specimens across the Atlantic for life in our country has been unsuccessful. Along with the birds, Mr Mann sent two or three local beetles. They were all prettily coloured but the eye was almost dazzled with the gem-like hues of the elytra of one astonishing beauty. It was about the size of our common Dor and would, I think, have made a lovely centre piece for a small brooch.

April (3rd) During the past few days the weather has been exceptionally mild and spring-like. The poor birds, after a severe winter, are now singing merrily, while the woods and fields are showing decided proof of returning animal and vegetable life . . .

June (1st) Our school report came today and is very good throughout – the lower standards being classed as nearly excellent. By the same post we got the sad news that our esteemed friend, Mrs Murdoch, late of Lynemore, has passed away . . .

July (10th) In several ways this has been a very pleasant day. During the afternoon three farmers' wives called at the schoolhouse, and gave me presents of butter, eggs and cream, together with a rabbit and a making of new potatoes. From a friend who is spending a short holiday on Ailsa Craig, Robert received a few botanical specimens gathered on the rock, along with a dozen of wild fowls' eggs, which he collected at some risk among the lofty crags for our cabinet.

(13th) We have in school a bright intelligent boy about nine years of age named Robert Masson, who has something so defective in his vocal organs that his own family are alone able, in some degree, to understand his very imperfect utterances. A short time ago my husband wrote to the directors of Donaldson's Hospital in Edinburgh explaining the condition of our pupil, and made application for him to be admitted into their institution. Today he was greatly pleased to have a letter from the secretary informing him that Robert is to be admitted as a beneficiary and will receive free board, lodging and education till he is fourteen years of age. To the little fellow this will be a great boon and I hope, in due course, he may be able to carn his own living.

(23rd) Our son came north on a visit to us for a few days and I was delighted to sec him looking so well and fit. The pony and trap, which he hired at Nairn for a little pleasure to us all, are to be kept by our good neighbour the Post. Robert brought me a dozen and a half of beautiful wine glasses, and a case of wine in order that I might have reason to use them . . .

(29th) Our son has now gone home again but has left his pony and trap with us for a few days, so that I might be able in comfort, to visit one or two friends who live at some distance from here. As my husband had to read a paper on Lochindorbh Castle to the Northern Scientific Societies at Forres, we both drove down and met a number of old acquaintances whom we had not seen since coming to Ferness. The story of the hoary ruin was well received by the various members who spoke at the close. Before leaving town I did some shopping and took up a pretty large hamper of provisions for our proposed picnic to the Streens.

Next Monday, though rather dull and sunless in the morning, the Young Men with their lady friends arrived at the Schoolhouse in nine machines. Having held a short conference, it was found that there was a difference of opinion as to the atmospheric conditions, but the 'weather-wise' asserted that it would clear up in a few hours and be a fine day. Providing ourselves, however, with suitable wraps, we all drove off in high spirits, Robert and I leading the long cavalcade. By noon we had run right under the huge cloud which hung low over the hills, and appeared so black and gloomy in the early dawn. The rain now fell in torrents giving the woods and fields along the water-side a very drenched and cheerless aspect. On arriving at our destination, we had to seek shelter in the farm steading at Knockandhu, where Mr and Mrs Macqueen did all in their power to make us as comfortable and happy as possible. After lunch and a good tea, our party had a very enjoyable dance in the granary while the rain cloud continued to pour down its watery contents, and the big drops beat more fiercely on the window panes with each returning shower-blast.

The Streens is a fine romantic Highland strath through which the Findhorn flows as a clear and placid stream. It is hemmed in on each side by a lofty range of undulating hills that rise so abruptly from the base towards the south, that for several weeks near the winter solstice, the people living at the homestead here do not see the sun even on a clear day. By the time we left, the river and its tributary burns, were in high flood, but our horses, having got a good feed and a long rest, took us back in a wonderfully short time considering the wet roads and the long distance that had to be gone over.

August (6th) For some days past Robert has been busy setting and arranging in suitable cases, a splendid consignment of Chinese insects sent to us from the Nairn Museum by Mr W Macleod, Hong-Kong, and late of Balchulchaich, Cawdor . . .

(22nd) When I left my bedroom this morning the sun had begun his appointed course in a cloudless sky, and by midday every bee, bird and butterfly were flitting about on lightest wing. Having had a note a week ago from Mr Donaldson stating that he wanted a clever lad as a clerk for the office in the British Linen Bank at Nairn, Robert went over to the Little Lyne to see if his old pupil, David Macglashan would be willing to apply for the situation. We have now got notice of the appointment and I trust this may prove the beginning of both a useful and prosperous career for the young man.

(23rd) Among a number of local flies which Robert caught last week on the Findhorn and sent to the Edinburgh Museum of Science and Art for identification, there was one which the entomologist Mr Grimshaw is sure has not hitherto been found in this country. The Lords of Committee requested him to say that should my husband 'care to part with his specimen, it would be a most welcome and valuable addition to their collection of British Diptera now being formed in the Institution'. This was willingly agreed to and the insect, *Chrysoclamys nigrifrons* has now been returned to the Museum. It is rather larger than the Common Cleg *Haematopota pluvialis*, with a black head and very beautiful wing nervation. The body all over is of a pale yellow colour with a bright metallic gloss – hence the generic name, meaning 'arrayed in a golden dress'.

September (2nd) Again Robert has been fortunate enough to fall in with another very rare fly. Of it Mr Grimshaw writes – 'I have to thank you for so kindly returning the specimen of *Didea [intermedia]* for re-examination . . . The specimen taken at Ferness is, so far as I know, the only capture in Scotland besides the one mentioned by

Mr Verrall [caught at Lairg]. The only other British record I can find is in a paper by the Rev. E.N.Bloomfield on 'Rare British Diptera in the British Museum', where he mentions the New Forest as a locality'.

(8th) Today Mrs Walker of Kinsteary drove up to the schoolhouse and in our absence, left a strange bird which had been shot by her gamekeeper. It turned out to be a Goatsucker or Nightjar *Caprimulgus europaeus* which stays here from May to September. In a letter thanking Robert for naming the specimen Mrs Walker wished him to keep it for our own collection. (23rd) The other evening while we were staying with the Rose family, a very fine specimen of a specially rare moth was captured by Bailie Baillie, Nairn, and sent over to Robert for identification. It was the Death's Head *Acherontia atropos*, fabled to cast from its wings a dust which produces blindness in those persons on whom it falls. After emerging from its chrysalis, probably in some neighbouring garden, the perfect insect had set out in the early twilight to enjoy life according to its natural instinct. Attracted no doubt in its flight by a powerful gas flare from an open window in Mr Baillie's house, it succeeded in making its way inside, and flew about the apartment greatly to the discomfort of the astonished inmates. After considerable trouble a tumbler was ultimately placed over it, and thus the mysterious intruder was safely secured in good condition. Under the influence of a few drops of chloroform it gradually sank into a comatose state, and finally closed its compound eyes in the sleep that hears no reveille. In the north of Scotland the Death's Head Moth is very rare, and the fact of its occurrence in Nairn is an additional proof of the general stability of the climate here. On the thorax there is a very conspicuous mark having a startling resemblance to a skull and the two collar bones which, combined with the feeble cry of the insect, caused it in bygone days to be looked upon as a mysterious visitant from spiritdom, and a sure 'harbinger of death, disease and famine' in the district where it chanced to be found.

(28th) On Saturday last a neighbour of ours, when returning from his work along the Grantown road near Logie Bridge, observed [and

Death's Head Hawkmoth

caught] a strange looking butterfly at rest on a low grassy mound under the trees . . . Robert . . . at once identified it as the much-prized Camberwell Beauty *Vanessa antiopa*. This rare insect occurs so seldom even in England that it has at times been believed to have become extinct . . . The colour is a rich puce-brown, blended with deep purple, while the wings, which measure about three inches from tip to tip, are edged with a broad grey band just inside of which there is a uniform row of blue spots. This is a most interesting discovery for the parish of Ardclach.

November (24th) When it became known that our friend Mr James Sinton, gardener, was to leave Glenferness, there was a widespread feeling of regret in the district . . . Tonight a deputation of gentlemen waited on him at his house and my husband presented him with a very beautiful time-piece, and a well-filled purse of sovereigns. Thereafter Robert also handed over to his daughter a handsome lady's bag along with a valuable travelling rug of Hunting Fraser tartan.

December (10th) This has been an exceptionally pleasant day for me. A good many dainty viands have found their way into my pantry, and in addition Lady Leven called to say farewell, and gave me a very pretty Shetland shawl. Our kind friend Mademoiselle Schneider [a visitor to Glenferness House] also looked in and handed us a large box of chocolates as a parting gift before going south. For all this I desire to be humbly thankful. (25th) This is an ideal Christmas day with the sky overhead quite blue and crystal clear as at midsummer. Two or three inches of snow fell during the night and at present the thermometer indicates several degrees of frost, but I am indulging in the luxury of a roaring fire which makes us very comfortable in our own little home. Starting during the forenoon Robert, in the course of a fairly long round on the Ferness side of the river, managed to visit fourteen different families, offering them the compliments of the season. On returning for a somewhat late dinner, we chaffed him that after receiving at least a dozen of drams, it would be imprudent for me to let him again pledge the wine cup even at his own table to drink the health of his nearest and dearest.

Camberwell Beauty

1897

February (1st) The temperature has been gradually falling for a few days past, and at night, when the sky was clear and unsullied, the twinkling stars came out in thronging multitudes to enliven the scene. Slowly however, the fair expanse became densely overcast, and the massive clouds began to empty themselves in a continuous snowfall which very soon laid the whole landscape under a thick and glittering mantle of spotless white. In consequence, the flowers of the field appear to lie dead, while it must be specially hard on the feathered tribes to have their scantly supplies almost entirely cut off for an indefinite period. The trees and hedges, being stripped of their summer verdure, are all richly draped with a lovely garment of the purest material, and our window panes all inlaid with a beautiful encrustation of many varied and highly artistic forms.

March (1st) Miss Annabelle Rose, a farmer's daughter in Tomnarroch beside us, has had several letters from a young man, a native of Ardclach and now in Manitoba, making her an offer of marriage. Though she only knew him as a boy in school with herself some twenty years ago, the literary wooing has just terminated to the satisfaction of both parties. In a few days she will leave Liverpool to consummate, on arrival, a rather hazardous union. When her gallant cavalier meets her at the appointed station on the Canadian and Pacific Railway some six miles from her new home, they will only recognise each other from their respective photographs, or by each displaying by arrangement, a coloured handkerchief. I wish her however, every happiness in her altered condition of life.

May (24th) On this day thirty-five years ago I experienced perhaps the greatest joy of my life, when I freely gave my heart and hand to the young man I most admired. There were several other candidates, farmers' sons who, at the time seemed very promising lads with every prospect of being comfortably settled in due course on their respective family holdings. In looking back however over a somewhat lengthened period, I note that one of my gallants was cut off by death soon after our marriage, and that each of the other three, proving a complete failure in business matters, sooner or later came to grief and had to leave the parental home. In my allotted sphere, we have been spared to each other while our mutual love and devotion have been retained in growing measure even amid the many family cares and anxieties quite inseparable from domestic life. But what my own condition would have been, had I become the wife of any one of my other lovers, I fear to think.

June (21st) Today Queen Victoria has completed her sixtieth year on the British throne, and the happy event is being celebrated with much enthusiasm all over the kingdom. Our church bell was rung at noon, and a few bonfires are to be lighted on the highest summits this evening at ten o'clock . . .

Ferness School Log Book: June 22nd – a holiday for the Queen's Jubilee.

August (1st) The early part of this day was hot and sultry, with mountains of ominous clouds slowly rolling together from every direction all over the sky. By the afternoon we were in the midst of a severe thunderstorm. While standing at the door a very bright lightning flash entered the ground quite near, and almost immediately after, we heard in the middle of the relative peal, a loud crash as if our house had been struck. We soon found that, happily, no damage was done. Then followed an exceptionally heavy shower of hail which, in its fierce madness did not last long, otherwise I feel sure our windows, like several of our neighbours, would have been broken. At first the hailstones were oblong masses of compact clear ice, each weighing fully an ounce; but afterwards they came down more peaceably in size and shape very similar to boys' marbles. (12th) Elsie and I made a nice fruit cake and sent it to Robert's aunt, Mrs Janet Adam, née Urquhart in Midmar on her ninety-sixth birthday.

August (30th) Robert bought a very quiet horse, six years old from Mr Anderson, Refouble, and paid £30 for him. We ought now to be greatly convenienced in going both to church and market seeing that we have a pony and machine of our own. They are to be kept at the New Inn by the farmer, Mr Maclean.

Ferness School Log Book: 15 October – There was a very disagreeable smell on the 13th inst. from the sewage drain through the waste pipe into the Boys' lavatory. 22nd – Airdrie children off with Scarletina. 29th – blockage of sewage pipe cleared. 5 November – three Aitnoch children kept off to avoid contagion with the Airdrie children.

December

Ferness School Log Book: 23rd – 16 degrees of frost. Mistress off with a severe cold and several children off.

(24th) Today the ground is just white with snow, and the frost, though extremely keen, is pleasant and quite invigorating. This has been a red-letter day to me. I got a beautiful cashmere dress and a large roll of spiced beef from my son. The neighbours too, have been exceedingly kind, having sent in two mountain hares, a large cut of fine home-fed pork, and a big bag of good potatoes, together with eggs, butter and cream . . . (25th) On this Christmas morning we received a very kindly letter sparkling with many reminiscences of his early experiences when quite a youth in Nairnshire, from the Rev. I.M. Campbell, D.D., Ph.D., minister of Pawnee City, Nebraska. He was one of Robert's first scholars after he came to Cawdor and he remembers him as an exceedingly diligent and promising boy . . .

(30th) Not less interesting was a letter from Mademoiselle Schneider written at the foot of Cheops, the largest pyramid . . .

1898

February (16th) During the past fortnight a good deal of snow has fallen but, with a slight rise of temperature, the roads have become very slushy and disagreeable with the result that our village might be looked on as a kind of hospital. In the evening I called at every house, and in each found a young invalid more or less ill, with one or two indeed requiring medical treatment.

March (2nd) My husband's aunt, Mrs Janet Adam, died yesterday at the Braes of Midmar. She was in her ninety-seventh year, and the remains are to be interred in the local parish churchyard . . . the first proofs of my husband's book 'The Natural History of a Highland Parish' came today, and we are well pleased with the size and type which have been selected.

April . . . (9th) Early this morning I was sent for to see Mrs Masson, who has just got the eighth addition to her family – all sons.

May (11th) This was our annual school examination day, and a cold wet one it was. Mr Macleod, H.M.I., had no ladies with him, but he was very pleasant with the children and everything passed off to our greatest satisfaction. In the morning I got several presents – cream, eggs, and a fine cut of pork.

Ferness School Log Book: Inspector's report – 'Mr Thomson who is a practical botanist, might profitably take the pupils occasionally to the woods and fields for instruction in his favourite subject.'

(25th) Elsie and I made a baptism cake for Mrs Masson's little boy who is to be called after myself, Richard Thomson Masson.

June (14th) The morning dawned with huge masses of dark clouds floating above the horizon. An hour or two later, after a heavy shower of unusually large drops, the sun shone out again bright and clear while the air felt refreshingly pleasant and bracing. Our school report, which is very good, came in the afternoon and Robert, as an experienced botanist, has been asked by the Department to take the upper classes at his discretion, to the neighbouring woods and fields, to give them practical lessons on plant life from living specimens found in their natural habitats.

Ferness School Log Book: 24 June – an hour spent in the woods looking at plants. Children were greatly interested . . . again on the 12th August – the scholars were much pleased.

August (1st) A very windy day and in consequence, clouds of dust are flying along the road. Not a little has silted into the several dwellings by the wayside, thus causing considerable additional trouble and annoyance to the tidy housewife. Mr Miller from the Established Manse, examined the school in Religious Knowledge, and expressed himself as very well pleased with the appearance which the children had made in the various subjects . . . This week I made and gave away several pots of red and black currant jam to my neighbours and friends. In the evening there were a few callers at the schoolhouse, and I received a beautiful piece of honey comb, as well as a large salmon caught in the river nearby.

(17th) Early in the afternoon the Rev. Patrick N. Playfair, M.A., minister of Glencairn in Dumfries, drove up in a nice landau and asked if Robert was at home . . . While perusing our list of the Ardlcach plants in the Transactions of the local Field Club, he had noted one or two specimens which hitherto he had not found. Having a spare afternoon he resolved to take a run to Ferness and gather them himself in their natural habitats. Accordingly Robert and he went down to the Levrattich bend of the Findhorn where they found *Juncus balticus* and *J. obtusiflorus* on a small boggy spot near the water's edge. A rare *Carex* was also added to the collection from a swampy hollow in the Tomnarroch burn. After their return, an hour or so was spent in looking over the specimens in our herbarium . . . We greatly enjoyed our short social intercourse and felt pleased that we had been able to make an interesting addition to his private collection.

September (10th) . . . Lady Leven called here this afternoon and invited us to her children's party at the Mansion House on Tuesday next. Robert sent a short article to the 'Nairnshire Telegraph' about the spots which are at present appearing unusually large on the solar disc . . . After having attended to several domestic duties which had been left over till the autumn vacation, we went down to Nairn for a fortnight's holiday, and as usual received a very cordial welcome from our good friends at 28 High Street.

(20th) The other day a serpent was killed in Waverley Road, Nairn, and being of unusual size and appearance, was sent up to my husband for identification. On examination it turned out to be a fine specimen of the Grass Snake *Tropidonotus natrix*, whose distribution has hitherto very doubtfully extended into Scotland. How therefore, this enterprising individual had managed to make its way so far from home, appeared rather puzzling. Perhaps, Robert suggested in the 'Nairnshire Telegraph', it was simply a railway excursionist that had come to enjoy the season in the popular 'Brighton of the North'. To this the Editor replied – 'Our esteemed correspondent is quite right. We now find that the Grass Snake was procured in the south, and was kept by a gentleman in Nairn for his amusement. It had managed to escape on the morning of its capture and despatch'.

1899

January (4th) The other day we were greatly interested in the ordinary bustle and industry of an ant hill in the wood nearby and Robert, in an article to the 'Nairnshire Telegraph' observed . . . that the one best known in Nairnshire is the Wood Ant *Formica rufa*, which as the trivial name implies, chooses the forest wherein to erect its large and intricate habitation. Above it is overlaid with numerous small sticks and pine needles, while underneath there is a wonderfully connected set of rooms, galleries and corridors laid out after a well conceived plan . . . Our British ants . . . treat aphids, or plant lice, in a very wonderful manner. Travelling long distances, they search for them, and as Linnaeus observed, even keep and protect them so as to feast at leisure upon their sweet secretions. This substance, when deposited upon the leaves of plants, was known to the Ancients as Honey Dew, and believed to be an emanation from the stars. These 'cows' are regarded by the intelligent [ants] as their own peculiar property, and they will defend them at all risks against the attacks of any foreign power. Occasionally they may be seen tapping and tickling some refractory individual with their antennae, inducing them to yield their saccharine 'milk' in order that they may either enjoy it themselves, or carry it off as a delicious repast for their hungry little ones.

Ferness School Log Book: late January – snow, roads blocked. Also in late March. May 16th – 19 boys and 21 girls present in school.

May (14th) Our neighbour Mr Maclean, and Robert went along to the farm at the Mount to have a look at the young cows with the view of buying one for me at the sale. There was a heavy thunder shower in the afternoon but they both reached home with only a slight wetting . . . (17th) At the roup today, Robert bought a fine black polled cow, called 'Tilda', for which he paid £12–2–6. In the evening I went over to see her at the New Inn where she is to stay, and think she will prove a great comfort to us. (24th) A branch telegraph office was opened this morning at Ferness, and as Elsie was about to start for Edinburgh, we had the honour of sending away the first message. It was addressed to our good friend Mademoiselle Schneider, now in residence with the Earl of Leven and Melville at Holyrood Palace, and it ran – 'Second John first and twelfth, Thomson'. On its delivery considerable difficulty, strange to say, was experienced among the officials of the Lord High Commissioner in finding a New Testament wherein to read the verse! However one was ultimately found, and Elsie was met in due course at the station. Then followed a good meal in one of the historic apartments near where Rizzio was torn from Queen Mary's side and cruelly murdered at the head of the stair.

Some weeks ago we had a letter from Mr Moir, Bombay, informing us that he was about to forward a small parcel, which I was to open, make a selection for myself, and then transmit the remainder to Robert at Hawthornlea. For a few days we were greatly exercised as to what the contents might prove to be. Today however, a couple of boxes, insured for £10, were handed in by the post and, much to our surprise and delight were found to contain a double solid silver tea service. The design on each was indeed beautiful and left almost no room for us to make a choice. We appreciate them very highly, and I have no doubt my son will do the same, when he sees the very dainty articles we have set aside for him.

June (9th) . . . Mrs Maclean, New Inn, sent me a fine pheasant which had got caught in one of their rabbit traps. In the afternoon we asked her to send over our cow 'Tilda' to eat up some rich grass in the garden, but having left her alone for a little while, found that she had broken through a weak part of the fence and eaten up most of our cabbages, at the same time trampling over the carrot and leek beds. It was indeed very provoking but there is not help for it now . . .

Ferness School Log Book: 28 July – The Junior and Senior sections had a visit to the neighbouring woods and examined many specimens of wild flowers and other objects of natural history. One boy found a female specimen of Cossus ligniperda.

The Natural History of a Highland Parish: – A worn female specimen of this moth was found by Johnnie Mackenzie, Ferness, in the wood which skirts the playground on Monday 12th July 1897 [sic?]. He gave it to me and the next day she laid her clutch of eggs on the drying board. The author has seen half-grown larvae (2 years old) feeding under bark of birch trees but had failed to catch an adult specimen.

August (10th) This morning one of our scholars brought a few wild flowers to school for the 'maister', and called his attention to a beautiful blue plant which he had gathered in a field near the Mains of Glenferness. There was very little difficulty in settling that it was a good specimen of Chicory *Cichorium intybus*, but as Nairnshire is considerably beyond the limits of its natural area, it is probable that a stray seed may have been conveyed to this district among a local consignment of grass seed from the south of England. As the species was in full flower and appeared to be in a healthy condition, it might be worth while for some enterprising farmer to try a crop as an experiment towards the solution of an almost chronic state of agricultural depression . . .

(23rd) For several summers past an unknown writer, during his annual holiday to the Brighton of the North, has been in the habit of sending a most interesting weekly contribution – The Diary of a Visitor – to the 'Nairnshire Telegraph', under the nom de plume of 'Ajax'. For long, the surmises among all classes here as to this gentleman's identity have been endless but as yet to no purpose.

Mr Bain the Editor, says the secret is one which he 'would not tell to the wife of his bosom!' Nevertheless the other day, when overflowing with good humour, he incautiously let fall the statement to my husband that Ajax was a London barrister, though that crumb does not go far to satisfy a hungry curiosity. Not a little, therefore, to our surprise did we learn from the 'Telegraph' of last week that this mysterious individual along with a scientific friend had been spending an afternoon with us here at the schoolhouse. He writes –

Went to Ferness by the Ardclach road with a fellow cyclist. Examined a curious bell-tower on top of a hill, the church being in the valley below. Told by a woman that it was due to an earthquake having 'let Down' the church. Puzzled over this, but could not reconcile it with the evidences on scientific grounds. Accosted by a herdboy with the usual question, 'What o'clock is it?' Understood he wanted to know the time of day, and in return for the information asked him about the tower with the bell. 'The wife you were speaking to is daft. Nobody here kens about them things but the schoolmaster!' Interviewed with fear and trembling the teacher referred to later on and found his explanation much more rational, and himself a most agreeable, intelligent man who told us all about the bell and a hundred other things. My companion and he had kindred tastes in the matter of butterflies and moths. Recommended us to try the banks of the Findhorn in the shades of evening, mentioning some rare species of moth to be found there. It was the only unwise thing he said. For no persuasion of mine would induce my friend to pursue our intended journey to Dava. Had to return with him to the river. Net in hand, he made some spendid captures. So he said. Having no interest in the matter, I strolled up the river. Came across a weathered slab bound with clasps of iron, bearing mysterious emblems and figures. Made a rough sketch. Found my companion had a copy of the Guide to Nairn and learned that the stone had a romantic legend attached to it – a Danish Prince and Celtic Princess, fugitive lovers, having been drowned at this spot in attempting to cross the river. Pursued my walk and came to the finest part of this most picturesque of all Scottish rivers – the Rock Walk. It is really charming. Have seen nothing like it anywhere. While my friends were engaged in their work of destruction amongst the insects with painted wings. I enjoyed to the full a ramble along this walk wondering how many of the visitors at Nairn had ever seen it – one of the loveliest spots in creation . . .

(28th) This morning Mr James Moir of Bombay, my husband and I left Aberdeen for Uddingston, crossing on the way both the Tay and Forth Bridges. The former is now a substantial structure, two miles long, but we could not help associating it with the terrible disaster on the 28th December 1879, when a great part of the first erection, bearing a passenger train, was thrown into the river during an exceptionally severe storm of wind. The latter, one and a half miles in length, over the estuary at the narrowest part, is probably the largest and finest bridge in the world . . . On our arrival in Edinburgh my son met us at the station and we all four had dinner in a fine hotel nearby. Thereafter we set out for Hawthornlea which was reached by five o'clock. During our stay we had a drive to Hamilton Palace but, as the Duke was in residence, our movements were somewhat restricted . . . Next evening we had supper with the Rev. John McIntosh in the Established Church manse, and as he is a Nairn boy, went to hear him preach on the following Sunday.

October

Ferness School Log Book: 6th October – 29 children present, late harvest and some children late in attending.

. . . (10th) Our friend Mr James Moir was married today in Aberdeen to Miss Charlotte Clarke. We sent a cheque for £5 to the bride, a telegram at the hour of the ceremony with our congratulations to both, hoping that they might be long spared to each other, not only for a short period in India, but especially in this country after their return from Bombay. (20th) During the past week the sunsets have been magnificent beyond the usual. Last evening in particular the purple hills along the western horizon stood out sharp and clear before the luminous glory of lovely rose, opal and faintest blue, as the Lord of Day sank to rest behind an archipelago of cloud, which floated serenely on the confines of an ocean of light. The splendour of the vision however, gradually became faint and more faint until approaching Night insensibly threw her dark curtain over the sky and left the spectator to enjoy in mental perception one of Nature's grandest displays of omnipotent beauty.

(28th) This was a lovely day and Robert and I had a long walk in the afternoon by field and woodland. We observed with some regret that the wild flowers were now a vanishing quantity, and have lost much of their summer charm; but as the golden Autumn steals over the forest trees they often put on, in their last hours, those ethereal robes which, tinged in a thousand dyes, set them forth in a grandeur which rivals even that of early spring. Generally the foliage by this time is a russet brown with purplish hues, though each member of the grove has its own distinctive shade which varies considerably with every stage of decay. Then comes Winter in all his boreal sternness but even he fails to rob the woods of their inherent beauty, for the advent of snow often serves only to array each twig and branch with a pure fleecy garment which emulates in another form even the pomp of their summer verdure itself.

November (3rd) Today we had a letter from both Mr and Mrs Moir, bidding us all farewell just before stepping aboard their steamer at the London docks on their way to Bombay . . . For some days past, I have been much troubled with my breathing, especially when I require to go up an incline . . . (17th) . . . Lady Leven called here in the afternoon and stayed for fully half an hour chatting freely over our local botany, and several other interesting parish affairs. She left a florin and asked Robert to give a prize of one shilling to the most polite boy and girl in school. (22nd) The Transvaal Boers, having rejected all attempts on the part of the British Government to secure a satisfactory settlement of the long standing grievances of the Uitlanders, presented their ultimatum on the 9th of October last and followed it up by an outburst of the terrible war now raging. Already there is much suffering among our soldiers in the upland wilds of Cape Colony, and Elsie was out collecting funds on behalf of their wives and families. Brodie of Brodie, Lord Thurlow, and Earl Cawdor have each lost a dear member of their respective households on the battle field while bravely fighting the enemy, and thus sorrow and sadness have suddenly become the portion of at least three well known houses in our neighbourhood. I hope the Powers may be soon able to arrange peace.

(19th) The late Rev Dr Gordon of Birnie had asked Robert in connection with his natural history pursuits in the Province of Moray, if he could find a genuine specimen in Ardclach of the ancient British 'Rottan', or black rat *Mus rattus*? After interviewing a number of local farmers on the subject, a full grown melanic vole *Arvicola ater*, was sent to the schoolhouse in the hope that one had actually been found. For many centuries the black rat was the only species in this country, but is now probably quite extinct . . .

December (2nd) For December this was a very fine day being clear and mild throughout. Mademoiselle Schneider from Glenferness and Elsie left here at ten o'clock on their bicycles for Nairn where they are to stay with our friends the Roses until Monday. My neighbour Mrs Masson called in the afternoon and gave me a photograph of her youngest son Dick Thomson, who was named after myself. In the evening we had a long letter from Mrs James Moir stating that she and her husband, although both somewhat advanced in life, had arrived safely at their future home in Bombay after a very pleasant voyage . . . (6th) As this had all the appearance of being an exceptionally wet day Robert sent Elsie a telegram in the morning asking her to engage a covered conveyance from the hotel for herself and friend, but on no consideration would the latter agree, and in consequence they both arrived this afternoon all drenched with rain. Otherwise the visit was very much enjoyed, Mr and Mrs Rose being exceedingly kind.

(10th) Mademoiselle was here early this afternoon. As usual she was very bright and does not seem to be in any way the worse of her weary ride from town under one continuous down pour of rain and sleet. She got three pounds of our Indian tea for her mother in

Lorraine, and Elsie made a nice cake and enclosed it in the same box as a small present from us. After she left, Lady Leven and her daughter Lady Betty called to say goodbye and expressed themselves as very sorry leaving our quiet locality and fine pure air for the interminable din and bustle of London. (17th) A few days ago an obscure member of Parliament asked the Prime Minister if he would be willing to telegraph from time to time, the progress of the Boer War to the various post offices for the information of the people in general over the country. This he agreed to do, and accordingly we now have any important news from the front at our very door in a few hours. Today I am sorry to see that there has been a rather serious British reverse in which many of our brave soldiers have lost their lives. Again it has turned out that a despised enemy has proved to be a rather formidable foe. (20th) An Uddingston family with whom Robert appears to be on very intimate terms, has been collecting various articles both useful and ornamental for several weeks past, on behalf of the families of our soldiers and sailors who are engaged in the Boer war . . .

(25th) During last weekend the Winter King duly arrived and, as snow was falling rather heavily at the time, I expected that the ground would be very soon covered to an inconvient depth. Last night however, a sharp frost set in and this morning the cold is intense; though to a healthy person the air feels crisp and even pleasantly invigorating. For many years it has become customary on this festive occasion for loved ones to feed the fires of good will and gaiety by sending to each other mutual greetings in the shape of illuminated cards to those whom they adore both at home and abroad. Today the postman brought me a number of beautiful specimens for which I am gratefully thankful. From Mademoiselle Schneider's mother in Lorraine I received a bottle of excellent brandy while my son sent me a case of port wine, along with a few other useful articles to fill up the box. In the afternoon a bottle of champagne from an Edinburgh friend and a beautiful black Shetland shawl from Lady Leven, were handed in to me. At six we go over to dine at Achagour when we expect to meet one or more friends at Mr Pryse Mackillican's hospitable board. Then after our brief relaxation from professional duties, we hope again to reopen school on the second day of the new year.

Ferness School Log Book: 27th–12 inches of snow. 28th–14 inches of snow. 29th–15 inches of snow.

(30th) There was a long telegram this forenoon from which it appears that General Cleary has gained a rather good position from the enemy, but at the cost of much bloodshed on our side. An old scholar, James Rose, Ferness, has a well written letter in last week's 'Inverness Courier', giving several interesting details of his military experience in the Transvaal . . .

1900

Ferness school Log Book: early January – 50% attendance.

February (1st) Snow fell continuously all last night and now the frost is very keen. As my health has been much below par for some weeks past, I had to remain in bed all day and several of my neighbours were at the schoolhouse asking for me. They brought me two large pieces of venison but it is doubtful if I will be able to enjoy it as I would like to do. (4th) More snow has fallen, leaving the roads almost impassable. I had rather a bad night, and my husband wired for Dr Adam, Forres, who arrived with some difficulty by sleigh about one o'clock. He examined me carefully, and found that there was an accumulation of serum all over my body just under the skin together with a weak heart.

Ferness School Log Book: 9th – influenza epidemic. Mistress and about a dozen scholars in village all in bed.

(11th) Our son came today and met Dr Adam in the afternoon. They both examined me and thereafter held a private consultation as to the exact nature of my trouble and about medicines suitable in my case. Before leaving for the south, Robert told us that he had decided to put another storey on his own house at Uddingston and so make ample room for us all to live together. Although somewhat taken by surprise we trust that this generous proposal may turn out for the best. There was a visitor here from every house in the village and in the evening I got a very handsome piece of woven material from Mr John Macdonald, India, and am sure it will make a most lovely tea cosy. (21st) In a letter from Edinburgh, our old scholar, Rachel, expresses her sorrow for my poor condition and wishes to come to Ferness and nurse me. This evening I had a parcel from Robert with some very old whisky and special medicines which I hope may prove of some service in reducing the abnormal swelling which has appeared in both my limbs. Yesterday our cow 'Tilda' had a fine calf at the New Inn, and in consequence Mrs McLean says we may now have an extra supply of milk should we so desire. Several neighbours have been here today asking for me. By special messenger, Lady Betty and her brothers sent me a large bouquet of beautiful flowers from Glenferness Gardens. Their kindness cheered me much, though my breathing is still very troublesome.

(24th) After a long spell of intense frost we were much pleased to find that a decided thaw had set in, when to our great consternation a leaden pipe upstairs suddenly burst in the evening and the water came pouring down on our furniture all over the parlour. Fortunately it was quite clean, but we had to dismantle the room and take up the carpet in order to get everything properly dried. Dr Adam, in passing, called and thinks there is some improvement, but my legs are still very much swollen . . . (28th) This was a fine day and I sat out for a short time in the warm sunshine to enjoy the fresh air. Doctor Adam called in the afternoon and put me on a new course of medicine which he thinks will soon have a beneficial effect, but the skin on both my legs has now broken under the knees and a watery fluid is oozing out very freely making me often feel rather uncomfortable . . .

March (1st) Our postman arrived at noon in high spirits with the Union Jack flying on his machine in honour of General Cronje's surrender to the British Army . . . (23rd) Mr George Bain, Editor of the Nairnshire Telegraph has just sent us the first proof sheets of my husband's little work – 'The Natural History of a Highland Parish', and thinks it may be ready for publication towards the end of the present year. Those who have read over the manuscript speak very favourably of the manner in which the various subjects have been treated. In later times, I hope the people of Ardclach may enjoy reading a description of much that doubtless will be considered old fashioned in their time . . .

April (3rd) Last night I was so uncomfortable in bed that I have decided to try and sleep in a sitting position on the couch. My system is much run down, but still, although my progress is undoubtedly slow, there is some improvement. In the afternoon I had all the scholars in seeing me: first the girls, and then the boys. I gave each one an orange and thanked them for so kindly inquiring about me everyday . . . Last night I had a pleasant sleep and felt much refreshed in the morning. (5th) About four o'clock a.m. I awoke with a severe pain in my chest. Elsie and Robert got up and put a hot poultice to my back and then gave me some brandy and laudanum which, in a short time, had the desired effect . . . There were so many people at the schoolhouse today that Elsie feels very tired and complains of a throbbing headache.

(8th) We have got the funeral letter of Alexander McIntosh, farmer, Levrattich, our late neighbour for several years when we lived in the old parish schoolhouse. Although a member of the School Board, there was very little love lost between us. Churlish and grasping in a high degree, he quarrelled during his lease with every family round his holding. Soon after we came to Ardclach, he wished my husband to exchange the rich grassy play-ground for an inconvenient piece of rough land on the hill side. This of course he could not do, but the refusal was to us a constant thorn in the flesh in connection with our scholars. When any of them ventured to take a short cut even over his unreclaimed land on their way to school, a serious complaint was sure to reach the 'maister'. Then came a prolonged and very irritating dispute with the School Board regarding the approach to what was originally the school well. We felt very glad, as far as he was concerned, when it was decided that we were to be transferred to the Ferness side of the river.

[*Ardclach School Log Book: 27th April 1877 – Mr McIntosh, tenant of Levrattich, has given notice through solicitors that he has an exclusive right to the Levrattich well. The schoolhouse has been supplied from it from time immemorial. The matter is under consideration by the School Board. 1st March 1878 – Workmen found water at a depth of six feet in the lower end of the play-ground, issuing from a bed of gravel and sand.*]

(24th) After a heavy rain fall during the night, the morning sun gradually beautified everything it shone upon and we had a lovely day. Robert was the presiding officer at our triennial School Board election . . .

May (9th) Yesterday was our Government inspection of the school. Elsie took my place on this occasion, and I was told that each class made a very creditable appearance. Mr Macleod, H.M.I. brought with him three lady friends . . . who spent most of the day visiting the interesting 'bits' of the Findhorn . . . After the children got away we all had dinner together and I greatly enjoyed the sparkling wit and humour at the table . . . (19th) Robert and Elsie drove down to Nairn for a few messages . . . Before returning my husband called on Mr Robertson, Chairman of the School Board and intimated to him our proposed resignation in the course of some months. He expressed his great regret and told us to remain until it was quite convenient for us to remove. The few special friends to whom we have confided our intentions, while congratulating us on our good fortune, have expressed their sorrow that my feeble condition should require such a change to be made. (21st) We have just had a letter from George Clarke Esq., C.E. informing us of his cablegram regarding the death of our most intimate friend Mr James Moir. He passed away very suddenly from suppressed small pox on the 19th inst . . . during the temporary absence of his wife on a visit to friends. After a long and happy acquaintance we can scarcely realize that his mortal remains have now been laid to rest for ever in a cemetery at Bombay so far away from his own native land . . .

June

Ferness School Log Book: 5th June – Mrs Thomson returned to work.

(5th) The Boer War still dragged on even after the surrender of Cronje, and has already cost the nation an enormous price in both blood and treasure, but I hope that the end is now in sight. We had a telegram from Robert this morning announcing the fall of President Kruger, and a few hours later a wire from Mr Robertson, the Chairman of our School Board – 'Lord Roberts entered Pretoria yesterday. Give the children a holiday'. Of course the little ones were all delighted and greeted the good news with three hearty cheers in honour of the happy event. Curiously enough, during my husband's long professional career, this is the first occasion on which he ever received any instructions from his superiors, either to do one thing or another regarding the conduct of school affairs – everything being left entirely to himself. I got a pretty bunch of garden flowers from Glenferness in the forenoon and had a number of callers after midday. In consequence, the cup in my Pantry is truly running over.

(8th) Today I had a letter from my son with the information that he has now gone into the cottage where he is to stay during the time that the other house is being enlarged, and he expects that it will be ready for us about the end of October. At a meeting of the School Board this afternoon our letter was read, and the members . . . agreed to 'accept Mr Thomson's resignation, and record their regret that, on account of failing health, he and Mrs Thomson should have to resign their charge, and they express the hope that, after such long and faithful service they may have many years of well-earned rest before them. (signed) Wm.Murdoch, Clerk' . . .

Ferness School Log Book: 15th June – Inspector's Report – Mrs Thomson, who used to assist in the school, has been unwell for some time and unable to attend to the work. There is in consequence a falling off in the results and Mr Thomson himself has not the vigour of former times . . . Nature knowledge is not properly graduated as between the two divisions of the school, but the Botanical lessons to the upper division are very interesting and instructive.

July (10th) I had a delightful drive this afternoon and enjoyed it so much, as it was my first outing for the last six months. A neighbouring farmer called in the evening and asked if we were to sell our pony 'Bobbie', but we told him that a bargain had been nearly concluded with Mr Maclean of the New Inn . . . (28th) My husband has received a letter from the Education Department requesting him to get a medical certificate from Dr Cruickshank, Nairn, as a preliminary to granting him a retiring allowance. On his return from town, he gave me a fine piece of salmon and a parcel of sweets.

August (8th) On opening the outer door this morning we observed an adult sparrow in a cosy corner on the floor apparently sound asleep with its head behind its wing. None of us could think as to how it had found its way in. It no doubt had come to the conclusion that, for one night at least, it would be quite safe under our roof. It ran however, a considerable risk, for 'Don' our pussy, was known to have twice passed within a couple of feet but failed to notice it. Elsie gently lifted it up and setting it free, said that it took a short flight and then settled on the walk to hop about as if it had just come down from its usual roosting place in the hedge near by.

(10th) The year's session having now come to an end, we closed school for the usual vacation, and at the same time ceased work in our official capacity. In the afternoon we gave the children a nice tea with fruit and then, shaking hands with each, we bade them all a last farewell as they passed out. This is my husband's birthday and it is rather interesting to note that he began his professional career in the Newhills Free Church School near Aberdeen, exactly forty four years ago. Teaching no doubt, has many drawbacks, such as irregular attendance, wild animal spirits among the boys, and the trouble one has with the dullards, but our own experience, both in and out of school, has been all that we could have desired. As our annual examinations however, from year to year drew near, we invariably felt more or less nervous as to the result but now, I am glad to note that none of our five Inspectors – Scougall, Barrie, Robertson, Jolly and Macleod – ever sent us a bad Report. The School Board too, gave us an absolutely free hand in everything pertaining to educational matters, and the problem of corporal punishment which was exercising the members of other Boards near us was never mentioned. Nor do I think there was any need, since at no time when settling some juvenile delinquency, did we ever lose temper or utter in passion a single word which, later on, we had any cause to regret. One day an old friend in conversing with my husband regarding the vicissitudes of his professional calling remarked – 'Ah, Bob, you must allow that all through life your lines have fallen in pleasant places, for in fact you have never known that you were born', and I believe he was not far wide of the truth.

(13th) This was an ideal day with just the amount of wind which enabled me to enjoy a rather long drive in great comfort. During our excursion we called at Levrattich, Moss-side, the Post Office, Rehaurie, Belivat and Cairnglass, and found everyone so very interested in my partial recovery but at the same time expressing regret at our leaving. I am sure that I feel better of the fresh air and especially of the encouraging social intercourse which I so much appreciated, although I did not at any of the houses come out of my conveyance . . . (22nd) This was a very cloudy morning with continuous rain all day. Had a wire that Rachel and our friend Mademoiselle Schneider were to be here in the afternoon and, accordingly, Robert drove up to the Dava station to meet them. As Lord Leven and Melville arrived by the same train, and having room in his own carriage for one more, he insisted on taking our French lady under cover to the schoolhouse. Robert sent a large boxful of books to an Edinburgh stationer who agreed to buy them at his own valuation. In the evening an old scholar Ludovic Alexander, called to ask for me. He is now a successful merchant in the Scottish capital and we were all very glad to see him.

(27th) A severe thunderstorm passed over our district this forenoon. The lightning was exceptionally frequent and vivid. At Clunas, some five miles distant a shepherd on the hill was struck by the electric current. Death must have been instantaneous as the body was reduced almost to a state of pulp. To such an extent was this the case, that a coffin had to be brought to the spot before the remains could be removed for interment to the churchyard. Mr Munro the estate factor, looked in for a few minutes today and told us that a dozen teachers have sent in their testimonials and become candidates for our school. Mademoiselle Schneider and Elsie cycled to Nairn and then took a train to Invergordon for Poyntzfield where they enjoyed a short holiday, and returned with a large basket of delicious gooseberries and a cube of honey. We got the usual invitation to the Tenants' Ball at the Mansion House but do not intend to accept as I assume that all my dancing days have come to an end! In the afternoon Elsie made twenty pounds of cranberry jam which we intend taking with us to Uddingston.

September (8th) A local photographer took a view of our school buildings today and from the negative we expect that it will turn out a great success. I was able to go out for a long drive and called on a number of those friends who had been so mindful of me during my illness . . . (29th) The teacher elect from Mull on the west coast called here about 9 p.m. to have a look at his new home. At first sight he had the appearance of a shepherd lad in a rough tweed suit and knickerbockers. On entering, he paid no attention to the door mat, and sat on the chair beside me for some five minutes before removing his cap. Throughout our half hour's conversation he smoked his pipe, was very Bohemian in manner, and ill-fitted I thought, to take charge of the nice children we were leaving.

October (1st) My husband reopened the school today as the new teacher finds that it will be impossible for him to take up his duties here for some time yet. I am very thankful that my health permits me to give more or less help, although the attendance in the various classes will now for a week or two, be nearly up to the average.

Ferness School Log Book: 5th October – The Thomsons resumed here until November 19th when James Macpherson, late of Ulva Public School, Mull, commenced. 30 pupils and still increasing.

(5th) A farmer, who had occasion to be at the schoolhouse this morning for the purpose of registering the birth of a little daughter, brought me a fine gigot of mutton. Then came a parcel of fresh vegetables from Glenferness gardens, and in the evening we had a letter from Mademoiselle Schneider stating that a basket of home-grown plums was on the way from Lorraine for me, but addressed to our new home in Uddingston . . . We have now heard from Mr George Bain that the first edition of 'The Natural History of a

Highland Parish' is now ready, and that about one half of the copies will have to be immediately sent out to those who subscribed for them some months in advance. We are pleased to observe that the work has received very favourable commendation by the editors of the leading Scottish newspapers. I think the publisher too, deserves much praise for the excellent manner in which he has presented it to the public . . . Again I had a long drive to say farewell to a number of dear friends, and called at Dalnaheglish, Refouble, Milton and Drumlochan. Having to cross a rough mountain burn in which the water was running full and strong, our pony was rather unwilling to encounter the flood, but a young farmer came to our assistance and 'Bobbie' took us all over quite safely. We were very kindly received at each house and everyone expressed sincere regret that we were leaving, but hoped that the change would turn out for the best to us.

November (12th) Our new home is not nearly finished. The tradesmen have been greatly hindered in raising the walls and putting on the roof on account of exceptionally wet weather. The heavy rain has penetrated to the rooms on the ground floor and it was found necessary to repair practically the whole house. To us, all this has been a source of much anxiety in connection with our arrangements for the flitting. My husband, having been local Secretary and Treasurer to the National Bible Society for twenty five years, sent in his resignation, and proposed James Rose, Tomnarroch as his successor in office. Mr J Wallace of the High School, Inverness, wrote asking Robert to read a paper to his Field Club, but he had to decline as we expect to be in Uddingston by the date specified.

(16th) A few days ago we sent our annual remittance to Mr Barron in payment of our 'Inverness Courier' and mentioned the fact that I and my family in Meikle Geddes, had been regular subscribers from the start on 4th December 1817. Today we have a nice letter from the Editor enclosing receipt and stating that owing to our long connection, but especially in appreciation of the merits of my husband's 'Natural History of a Highland Parish', the 'Courier' will continue to be posted free of charge to our future address.

(17th) Under the Education Act of 1898 Robert has just received a letter informing him that their Lordships have granted him an annual Disablement Allowance of £44–1–4. Though a small sum, it is the highest which they could have awarded in accordance with the law as it stands at present. Thus all things considered, we have not reason to complain, seeing that previous to the passing of the above Act we had no claim, even on the liberality of our own Board. The Colporteur was here in the afternoon on his last visit before our removal and said he would miss us very much when on his usual rounds. We also regret parting with one whom we greatly respected. He has done much good work since his appointment in Nairnshire, especially among the young who eagerly read the high-toned literature which he brought to them from month to month. There was a note from the Editor of the 'Aberdeen Free Press', asking my husband for his photograph to appear above an article sketching his career in that paper. Again we had another parting with our scholars. This was no easy matter after more than a quarter of a century's residence among them. Many associations increased the reluctance we felt in leaving the old place. They all shook hands very heartily at the school door and wished us a good journey south.

(18th) This has been a red letter day. A deputation consisting of Messrs John Mann, John Murdoch, Thomas Simpson, Alexander Innes, farmers, along with the Earl of Leven's factor, came to the schoolhouse and presented us with a very handsome silver Fruit Stand which cost twenty guineas. Mr Mann, in handing over the gift, assured us that everyone in the district subscribed most cheerfully and deeply regretted our removal. In his reply my husband said that he felt extremely grateful for the complimentary manner in which each of the gentlemen present had been pleased to refer to our work in the parish. We have tried he added, to do our duty as best we could, and now it was a very great pleasure, when closing our professional career, to find that those whom we have served so long should come forward in such a generous way to express their good will and respect to us before leaving for the south . . . We shall always he concluded, be delighted to hear of the success and welfare of those who had been under our care both in the Parish and Ferness Public Schools.

(19th) This was a fine cold winter day which made the warmth and comfort of the house all the more appreciated. Mr Scott, carpenter, the Mount, of his own free will came and packed our furniture into the van which Robert sent from Uddingston. Our successor Mr Macpherson, called in the afternoon and bought our everyday chairs, tables and oilcloth. This was very fortunate as my son did not need them. My husband presented a large number of books to his friends, and sent a hundred weight to a secondhand bookseller in Edinburgh getting a small sum in return. In the evening we had a letter from Mr Kenneth Macrae, Headmaster of the Church Street School, Nairn, stating that the local Association of Teachers and others wished to entertain us to supper in the Royal Marine Hotel before leaving. Robert wired back that we were very grateful to our kind friends and would be delighted to accept their invitation. Twenty three people called at the schoolhouse today, and I feel rather tired after all the exertion I had to make, but was greatly pleased to see them all.

(20th) This morning we all bade a last farewell to Ferness. The furniture van left by rail in the evening, but we are to remain with our good friends the Roses for a few days in Nairn until our new home is out of the tradesmen's hands.

(28th) Tonight we were entertained to supper in the Royal Marine Hotel by the Nairnshire Teachers' Association and other friends. Mr Riach, Nairn, the President of the Branch, occupied the Chair, and among those present were Mr J Macleod, H.M.I.; Mr J S Robertson, Factor and Chairman of the Ardclach School Board; Doctor Cruickshank, M.D.; Mr Donaldson, Solicitor; Mr Bain, Editor of the 'Nairnshire Telegraph'; Mr Lobban, Rector, Nairn Academy; Mr Watson, Auldearn Schoolhouse; Mr Fraser, Campbell's School, Ardclach; Mr Allan, the Schoolhouse, Cawdor; Mr John Rose, Merchant, Nairn; Mr K Macrae, Beach Wood; Mr John Cameron, Rosehall; Dr Sutter, Nairn; Mr Jamieson, Carron Villa; Treasurer McIntosh; and Mr Wm Murdoch, Clerk of Ardclach School Board. Letters were read from Colonel Clarke, and Provost Dallas regretting their inability to be present.

After the usual loyal and patriotic toasts, Mr J S Robertson proposed the toast of the evening – the health of Mr and Mrs Thomson. In giving the toast he said that he was sorry it had not fallen into abler hands, to someone who had known Mr and Mrs Thomson longer than he had done, but this he could say, no-one could have a higher opinion of them, no-one could admire them more for the work they had done, or respect them more for the character they had shown, than he did. Mr Thomson had the almost unique record of having been forty four years in the teaching profession, and had never been a single day absent from school all that time, either from illness or any other cause. That said very much for the stuff that old teachers of our schools were made of and, without reflecting in the least on the younger generation, he doubted whether any of them, for the shorter period they had served, could show a record of that kind.

Mr Thomson began teaching in this district in the Free Church School at Cawdor in the year 1858. In those days they were not bothered with Education Codes or Inspectors and he did not think the work in school was any worse done on that account. In fact he thought that teachers were being unnecessarily trammelled and harassed by the excessive requirements of the Code and the constant changes in books and subjects under the present system. Teachers like Mr Thomson did not require these things. They could adapt their teaching to the circumstances of the pupils and the character of the district without the perpetual interference of idle clerks in Dover House [the then Headquarters in Whitehall, London of the Scottish Office]. Mr Thomson in 1874 removed to Ardclach, where he became the first teacher under the School Board.

As Chairman of the Ardclach School Board, [Mr Robertson] had frequent opportunities of coming into contact with Mr Thomson, and of knowing the work he was doing. As many of them knew, the School Board had some very difficult and delicate duties to perform and

Mr Thomson was in the course of the changes transferred from the old school of Ardclach to the new one at Ferness . . . The excellent work which he had done as a teacher was well known to them. They also knew the devotion of Mr Thomson to the study of natural history and the high position he had taken amongst naturalists of the country. He was glad to say that the fruits of Mr Thomson's lifelong studies were not to be lost to the world, for he had gathered them up and was about to issue them in a book. He was sure they all looked forward with great interest to the forthcoming publication of 'The Natural History of a Highland Parish' – the title chosen for his new work. In conclusion, he acknowledged the hospitality dispensed by Mr and Mrs Thomson during their sojourn in Ardclach, and the pleasure a visit to their home afforded. They were very sorry at their leaving the district, but wished them much happiness in their new home on the banks of the Clyde.

In reply my husband said he only wished he could return thanks for me and himself in words suitable to the very kind and far too complimentary terms which had been expressed . . . I have spent, he said, 42 years in Nairnshire, of which almost twenty seven have been in Ardclach, and during that long period we have received a free admission into not a few of the sacred precincts of domestic life. In several cases, both in Ardclach and Cawdor, our relations were so intimate that we occasionally felt that we had actually become members of these families, and among them we certainly formed some of the dearest friendships we shall ever enjoy on this earth. Everywhere we found a kindness and courtesy which has been greatly valued even to the present day. When I began teaching on the 10th August 1856, my birthday, in the Free Church School at Newhills, the educational methods were generally the same in every parish throughout Scotland. In those days it was not expected that every child could become a bright scholar, because it had to be acknowledged that Nature had decreed otherwise. Hence the children were not required to work under the same iron rule which was the practice in our Board Schools as directed by the Revised Code. In conformity with a process of natural selection the mental capacity of the most promising pupils was carefully nourished and stimulated by the judicious teacher, often in view of a possible University course. No doubt the plan had its defects, but all over Scotland it produced excellent results. Again, at the present time, there is a marked tendency at Dover House, to introduce modified changes on the more sensible lines of the old parochial system, and I am firmly of the opinion that the principle is sound, and certain to prove satisfactory.

Soon after I came to Cawdor, four dominies met in the early sixties one evening in the Nairn Parish Schoolhouse. They were the late Mr Penny, Parochial Teacher; Mr Donald Macleod of the Free Church Institution, Nairn; Mr John Macnaughton, Parish Schoolmaster, Cawdor; and myself. After talking over a few professional subjects, it was decided to issue a circular to the brethren in the presbytery suggesting the formation of a local teachers' association. This was done, and a few years later our body joined the parent society in Edinburgh, and was duly incorporated as a branch of the Educational Institute of Scotland. I am now the only survivor of the original quartet and, although on account of my later geographical position in the south of the county I was unable to attend all the meetings, I regularly paid the annual subscription . . .

Through life the Virginian weed had no attractions for me, and even the latest novel, however fascinating, seldom occupied more than a fraction of my time. But like the poet, I found a lasting pleasure in the pathless woods – an elevating society where none intrudes. The legends, the wild flowers with the bees, the butterflies, and other insects, presented me with an endless variety of design and purest delight. In Ardclach, so far as known to me, the field was all my own and therein I reigned supreme without anyone seeking to dispute my claim. In 'The Natural History of a Highland Parish', now almost through the press, I have tried to lay up in a permanent form many fleeting characteristics which, alas! could not have been done, had the work been delayed to the present day. For me this had been entirely a labour of love, and I shall feel amply rewarded if, through my instrumentality, future generations may be made to think kindly of the nineteenth century Ardclach.

In a few days we expect to open our eyes in a fresh environment, but that we may not forget the old familiar scenes and faces of our earlier years we have provided a series of local photographs to be kept as family treasures in our new home at Uddingston. Among these may I mention the former and present Schoolhouses, Dulsie and Logie Bridges, with the quaint Bell Tower and sacred churchyard. I am sure you will readily agree that it is something more than a wrench to leave behind the generous and kindly friends we have formed in Nairnshire, and to begin life as it were anew in an unknown community, but I can honestly say that the pleasant memories of our social life will not soon be forgotten, and we trust that our many esteemed friends may occasionally have a few happy recollections of us when settled in our adopted home on the banks of the Clyde.

In the course of the evening, Mr John Macleod, Her Majesty's Inspector of Schools said he had a very great pleasure in being present to do honour to Mr Thomson. He had found [him] a most excellent teacher and his school admirably conducted. Much however as he respected him, he might be permitted to say that he regarded Mrs Thomson as even better. He esteemed Mr Thomson, but he loved Mrs Thomson. This lady had really been a most able teacher and had done her part nobly, not only in the school, but in the district.

He also referred to Mr Thomson's work as a naturalist, and congratulated him on the position to which he had attained amongst students of natural history, and they would all cordially welcome his book. He wished them many happy years in their retirement near the great commercial metropolis of the west.

Other gentlemen spoke in similar terms of appreciation and acknowledged the hospitality afforded by Mr and Mrs Thomson to the members of the Nairn Literary Institute and others, on the occasion of their frequent visits to Ardclach and Ferness . . .

Transactions of the Inverness Scientific Society and Field Club, vol. VI (1899–1906) pp 207–208.

4 July 1902 – Mr Thomson, Uddingston, formerly of Ardclach – presented his natural history collection to the Nairn Literary Institute – comprising butterflies, moths, beetles, flies, several cases of foreign insects and about 200 birds' eggs from Ardclach representing about 80 species.

[The Inverness Museum still has some of these specimens.]

1901

Mrs Thomson's Last Illness

Born at Little Budgate, Cawdor, on the 28th of May 1841, and died at Hawthornlea, Uddingston, on the 18th of December 1901.

In the early months of 1900 my dear wife began to show the symptoms of Myxoedema . . . This, owing to a diseased condition of the thyroid gland, was accompanied by an oppressed breathing which became greatly intensified after the slightest physical exercise . . . After removing to Hawthornlea, Uddingston, in December 1900 [Mrs Thomson] was wonderfully well for almost the whole of the next year and was able on one occasion to visit the ruins of Bothwell Castle on foot. By the beginning of December 1901 however, the old symptoms began to recur, and Robert called in Dr Middleton, chief of the Western Infirmary, Glasgow, who prescribed a low diet and complete rest in bed. Her tonic medicines were again resorted to but without any favourable results, while her malady clearly gained in power from day to day . . . On Monday the 16th she expressed to me a feeling of general weakness . . . Henceforward she was often weighed down with sleep, but in the intervals appeared bright and cheerful, till the afternoon when unmistakable signs of approaching dissolution were clearly traceable in her face. Although familiar with such indications, I still refused to acknowledge their warnings, hoping even against hope. From this time onwards, it was with difficulty that we could manage to keep her awake, while giving her some spoon-food. In a lucid moment however, about nightfall, she opened her eyes and, speaking in a distinct tone, imparted a few wise counsels to us regarding our respective duties to each other both for the present and future world . . .

Early on Wednesday morning . . . she lay back on the pillow and quietly closed her eyes in apparent sleep. Neither on this occasion nor yet through her long and trying illness, did we ever hear one repining murmur fall from her lips. About an hour later her breathing became more oppressed, and after sinking into an unconscious condition, passed peacefully away in our presence at half past seven in the evening, some five minutes before the arrival of Dr Middleton and Robert from Glasgow . . .

The funeral was arranged for Saturday the 21st of December at 2 p.m. in the Bothwell Park Cemetery, a little over a mile from Uddingston . . .

Throughout her married life, she earnestly strove to discharge her incumbent duties with scrupulous fidelity, and found in them the highest satisfaction for her natural inclinations. Sweet and womanly at all times, she was a devoted mother and a true friend to everyone whom she received into her beloved circle. In the great majority of cases in which we took opposite sides on any particular question of public or private interest, she resolved the whole matter by an innate apprehension and gave her decision upon it. In this way I had on many occasions later on, to acknowledge her shrewd perceptions and own that she was in the right. From the first day we met in Meikle Geddes I greatly esteemed her, but did not realize how much I was actually bound up in her till the remains were laid to rest in the narrow house at Bothwell Park. The darkness however, is past and let me hope that the true light now shineth.

1916
December

My only son Dr Robert Thomson, having contracted a chill which developed into a sharp attack of pneumonia, died suddenly at his residence, Hawthornlea, Uddingston on Sunday afternoon, the 28th of November, aged forty-nine years and eleven months.

He was born in the Free Church Schoolhouse, Cawdor, Nairnshire, on the 30th of December 1865 and received his early training from myself, till he went to Rainings School, Inverness, where he studied for a year under the late Dr Macbean, the distinguished Gaelic scholar. In due course he completed his medical curriculm at the Universities of Edinburgh and Aberdeen, where he graduated with the degree of M.B.,C.M., when in his twenty fourth year.

While a student he spent a whale-fishing season in the Arctic regions as surgeon on board the steamship 'Resolute', Captain

Jackman, of Dundee. During this expedition his vessel was the most successful of the fleet, having secured 34,000 young harp seals, equal to 771 tons of weighed out fat and skins. After being capped in Marischal College, he made two voyages to Calcutta as doctor on board the Clan Line steamship 'Matheson' which was torpedoed and sunk by the Germans in 1915.

His connection with Uddingston began in July 1890 when he came to Tannochside as assistant to the late Dr McGowan, Bellshill, and in this capacity acquired a widespread reputation in the district. Three years later he commenced practice in the village on his own account, and soon afterwards assumed Dr J Carruthers as a partner. Among his professional brethren he rapidly became very popular and was generally recognised by his many patients as a skilful medical adviser and trusted friend.

As an instance of his energy and ability the year after he had settled in the village, he engaged a *locum tenens* and studied during a summer session at Edinburgh University. He came out top man in each of the subjects taken, at the same time handing over to the second man his gold medal, as a valuable recommendation for him in starting a professional career in his own district. He was one of the medical officers for the Parish of Bothwell, and had a seat on the Panel Committee of National Health Insurance. A few years ago his public services were recognised by the County authorities, and he was nominated and duly appointed a Justice of the Peace for Lanarkshire. Born in the schoolhouse, he naturally took an intelligent interest in education and was for five years a member of the Bothwell School Board, and Convener of the Uddingston Grammar School.

His mortal remains were laid to rest near those of his mother in the Bothwell Park Cemetery on Wednesday the 1st of December 1915. As the funeral cortege wended its way through the village, the crowds which lined the streets bore striking testimony to the respect in which he was held by all classes of the community . . .

11th April 1916

Minute of Kirk Session held on the 12th March 1916.
The Moderator submitted a letter he had received from Mr Robert Thomson intimating his resignation of his membership of the kirk session. The resignation was accepted with regret and Mr Thomson was thanked for his services in the post. It was also agreed to minute the session's high appreciation of these services, and the clerk was (signed) Thos. Robertson, Session clerk.

Nairnshire Telegraph January 23, 1923

The late Mr Robert Thomson of Ardclach.

We regret to announce the death of Mr Robert Thomson at Uddingston on Thursday last. He had been ailing for some time back, but his demise was unexpected. The greater part of Mr Thomson's life was spent in Nairnshire – first, as the teacher of the Free Church School, Cawdor, and next as the teacher of the Parish School at Ferness, Ardclach. In both spheres he proved himself a most successful teacher, and many of his pupils have risen to good positions at home and abroad, and will ever cherish fond memories of him both for his friendliness in intercourse and his thoroughness in his methods of training. He was a most worthy man in every relation of life. At an early period of his career, the deceased gentleman became an ardent student of natural history and excelled especially in knowledge of botany, recognised latterly as one of the highest authority in the North on that subject. He did not however confine himself to that branch of knowledge but interested himself in the folklore, place-names and antiquities of the district in which he had so long laboured, and some twenty years ago he gathered together the fruits of his study and research, and published them in a handsome volume, which he entitled 'The Natural History of a Highland Parish' (Ardclach). It was highly praised by the Press, being described as almost unique of its kind for the variety and interest of its contents. Mr Thomson's literary labours did not finish with the publication of his book – he continued to contribute up to the very end papers to learned societies and articles to the Press on a variety of subjects of a literary and scientific character. On retiring from the teaching profession, Mr Thomson removed to Uddingston, where his son Dr Robert Thomson was engaged in a large practice, but predeceased him some few years ago, as did his beloved wife who belonged to Cawdor. He is survived by his daughter, Miss Thomson for whom much sympathy is felt.

APPENDIX A

Essay on the County of Nairn by Robert Thomson and submitted to The Fine Arts and Industrial Exhibition at Nairn on 3rd September 1884. (Highly Commended).

THE COUNTY OF NAIRN

General characteristics.

Position: Nairnshire is one of the smallest counties of Scotland. It is situated between 57 and 58 degrees of northern latitude, is bounded by Elgin on the east and Inverness on the south and west, and forms part of the northern seaboard of the Moray Firth. Originally it formed part of the ancient province of Moray and covers an area of 215 square miles. It consists of one large and several small detached portions. This originated when the Thaneage of Calder, including . . . the barony of Ferintosh in Ross and several parts of Stratherrick, Strathnairn and Strathdearn, and a large portion of the lands of Glammis in the Mearns, were all politically . . . considered as pertinents of the Sheriffdom of Nairn.

Climate: It enjoys a climate of exceptional salubrity, combining the mildness of a marine temperature with the bracing influences peculiar to the moorland breezes. As the annual rainfall seldom exceeds 26 inches and the general character of the soil is usually porous, it is exceptionally free from fogs and other sources of a malarial nature. It has been truly remarked that 'Nairn and Moray enjoy 40 days more of summer weather than any other of the northern parts of Scotland.' The prevailing winds are westerly, but the superabundance of moisture which would otherwise fall from the rain clouds of the Atlantic is divided and passes along either the rugged margins of the great Caledonian Glen, or sails over the highlands of Banffshire.

Scenery: The maritime champaign for several miles along either side of the River Nairn presents a landscape of almost garden-like beauty. Viewed from the western vicinity of the Royal Burgh, the whole Strath appears prettily laid out in nicely sized farms, each with its substantial and adjoining villa-like family residence nestling among woodland patches which stretch on towards the southwest, till, towards the head of the valley, it culminates in an extensive grove of ancestral limes among which lie embosomed the grey turrets of the fine old baronial stronghold of Cawdor. This beautiful scene is relieved by brown heath which spreads out in the far background into a series of gentle undulations and extends away over the distant uplands until the boundary is lost in the thin blue of the descending horizon.

Agriculture: As an agricultural district, Nairnshire is unsurpassed in the North of Scotland. The soil is free and loamy and produces grain in never failing abundance. In addition to the ordinary cereals, wheat – though occupying a small acreage – attains a degree of excellence which entitles it to be ranked among the finest productions of the kind in Great Britain; if we remember that the sample grown by the late Mr MacKillican, Piperhill, was awarded the first prize at the International Exhibition of 1851. The barley too of Nairnshire fetches a high price in the London market.

Climate and soil are both highly favourable to horticulture, which is carefully and successfully practised. Peaches, apricots and nectarines ripen on the open walls in ordinary seasons and even figs and sweet almonds are occasionally matured. Flowers too, of species comparatively rare to these northern latitudes are here brought to perfection, and in particular are so worthy of notice that the Rose, 'the Queen of the garden', in all its varieties, as cultivated at Achreigh, has attained a reputation as wide as its exquisite beauty and delicacy of form so deservedly entitle it.

Forests: The forests of the county are both extensive and valuable and cover an area of 13,241 acres. Within the last fifty years considerable additions have been made to their extent, and in connexion with this it is worth noticing that the late forester, Mr James Black, on the Cawdor estates, received the gold medal at the Exhibition of 1851 for having transferred from the nursery to the woodland no fewer than 15,000,000 plants, chiefly fir, larch and oak. The principal conifers are the two former. Dulsie Wood has long been noted for the excellence of its natural timber and there are some magnificent specimens of larch on both the Cawdor and Lethen estates. The hard woods come next in importance and are chiefly oak, ash, elm, beech and birch. To the latter, the exceeding beauty of the landscape is indebted for those brilliant tints of lovely green which refresh and charm the eye in the early part of spring, as well as for that wonderful admixture of ever-changing colour which lends a special enchantment to the mountain slope and river margin during the late months of autumn.

Wellingtonia gigantea, *Auricaria embricana* and others from abroad have been introduced by the foresters with satisfactory results and are beginning already to impress with their peculiar effect the general aspect . . . of several of the country mansions.

Geology: The Lower Silurian is the prevailing Geological formation which consists chiefly of mica slate, gneiss and quartzose rocks. It occurs in most of the upland district along with small portions of granite which appear on the surface of Ardclach, and is also seen protruding through the overlying Old Red extending from Rait Castle to Kinsteary. The huge boulders found in the lower district are by many supposed to have drifted from the granitic patches along the Findhorn. Towards the coastline the superincumbent stratum is the Old Red Sandstone, which in the middle district consists of conglomerate . . . The junction between these two systems is clearly seen near Achniem on the Cawdor Burn, and other sections on the Findhorn, lying tilted rather perpendicularly on the subjacent gneiss. This deposit which has produced barren moors in other parts of Scotland, is in great part due to the rich soil of the lowlands of Nairnshire. From a finely grained layer in the vicinity, the builder obtains the material with which he has reared those handsome structures which adorn both the town and suburbs of the Burgh of Nairn.

At Braeval in Ardclach there are found in great numbers those limestone nodules which illustrate the peculiar ichthyology of the Old Red. It is interesting to remember that both Hugh Miller, the monographer of this deposit, and Agassize obtained some of their finest specimens of *Pterichthys*, *Coccosteus* and *Holopticheus*.

Soil: In the southern upland districts the soil is light and sandy, while low down in narrow glens especially along the Findhorn, small tracts of alluvial deposits lie like oases in the desert, beautifully fringed by alders, pines and birches. Beyond and on either side, the moorland stretches out into heathclad knolls and bens until it reaches the extreme boundary along the summit of the Monadhliadh range. These regions are chiefly pastoral and only in the less elevated portions does cultivated land exist, which increases in extent and fertility with descent towards the coast. The total extent of land under cultivation in the county amounts to about 26,000 acres. Of this cereals occupy about 9,200, green crops 4,700, grasses considerably over 10,000 while that under permanent pasture scarcely exceeds 2,000 acres.

Botany: Of the total number of wild flowers common to Great Britain, Nairnshire claims considerably over one fourth. The oak fern, beloved for its graceful form and delicate green colour, is generally abundant in many localities. The beech and shield ferns are well represented on the banks of the Findhorn. *Fragilis*, *Tricomanes*, *Lonchitis* and *Scolopendrium* occur in favourable situations. The curious moonwort is common in Ardclach. According to legend it was endowed with the power of opening locked doors, and even drawing the shoes from the feet of any horse which might be so unfortunate as to unwarily tread upon it. The fine water lily *Nymphea alba* flourishes in the Loch of Belivat and the graceful fairy form of *Trientalis europea* may frequently be met with on the moors. The leaves of the common Lady's Mantle is a special object of beauty if examined under water and its northern sister *Alpina* – on the underside of its serrated leaflets – rivals the most delicate productions of the loom.

Entomology: The district also presents a rich field for the researches of the entomologist. Situated as the region is, beyond the alpine heights of the Grampian range, it may be a matter of surprise to the more favoured student of natural history to learn that the list of Lepidoptera contains 20 different species of butterflies and about 120 moths. *Argynnis adippe* was taken for the first time last year at the schoolhouse of Ardclach, and a few specimens of *Vanessa cardui* captured in the same locality, settles the question that it too is a native. The splendid Emperor Moth *Saturnia pavonia minor*, the Fox *Bombyx rubi* and the great Oak Eggar *Lasiocampa quercus*, are frequent along the banks of the Findhorn. In short the variety of design combined with the beauty of colouring exhibited on the wings in a local collection is equal, if not superior, to larger and more gaudily coloured denizens of a warmer clime.

Ornithology: Among birds the much-prized Goldfinch is from time to time to be met with in the Glenferness woods. The Heron still continues to build occasionally on the Findhorn, and the eggs of the Little Grebe have been found in the Loch of the Clans, while the Black-headed Gulls (popularly 'Pickie Tars') breed in great abundance in the Lochs of Belivat and Highland Boath in Ardclach. Loch Loy is also a favourite resort of at least one pair of wild swans. The curious Crossbill, noted for its fearlessness of character, is plentiful among the fir woods all over the county, and the Rook and Wood Pigeon are so numerous as to have called forth of late the deadly enmity of the farmer against them.

The parishes.

Ardclach: This parish is the largest in the county. Its southern part consists almost entirely of moorland which in scattered portions still largely remains unreclaimed by the plough throughout its whole extent. The arable land is divided into medium and small-sized farms and crofts, to each of which is usually attached a large amount of pasture. The staple productions are oats, barley, turnips and potatoes. The moors support flocks of sheep and a few herds of Highland cattle while the adjoining solitudes contrive to be the retreat of great numbers of Red Grouse and other associated natives of the mountain and tarn.

The human population is 1,117 and there are 70 Parliamentary voters. The rental is roundly £7,000, the principal proprietors being Alexander Brodie (minor) of Lethen, and the Earls of Leven and Cawdor.

Through the south eastern side of the parish lies part of the course of the River Findhorn, a rapid and treacherous stream causing, especially in former days, many distressing accidents along its fords, but it is regarded by sportsmen as an excellent stream for both salmon and trout. On entering Nairnshire it winds through the deep and picturesque glen of the Streens. On either side precipitous cliffs rise sometimes almost from the water's edge, preventing in some places the direct rays of the sun from being seen for more than a few minutes during the short days in winter. A few stunted pines, blending their own sombre green with the grey rock and purple heath, are scattered over the adjoining acclivities, striking their gnarled and twisted roots deep into the crevices in search of nourishment, while on the lower slopes, birches and alders abound.

Further on the river plunges into a narrow chasm, where flowing deep and dark, hemmed in by steep rocks and spanned by the old military bridge of Dulsie, it forms a most beautiful scene. On the south side, close by, rises the hill of the Doune, with its peculiar tabular summit and smooth wooded sides. From its top an extensive and interesting view can be obtained; and in ancient days, although no vitreous markings are visible, it must have afforded an important link in the chain of beacons along the Findhorn while, according to the folklore of the district, it was a favourite fairy retreat.

In the immediate vicinity of Glenferness House stands a runic stone, which the legend says was erected to commemorate the death of a princess who, with her Danish lover, perished in the adjoining stream in their endeavour to elude the hot pursuit of her irate father. The river is continued to Daltullich through a stretch of the most varied scenery and passes the parish church with its ancient graveyard, while the Manse and Belfry stand in the immediate vicinity at an elevation of nearly 200 feet above the bed of the stream. The following acrostic, recently (1883) composed, aptly describes the scene:-

Findhorn! there is magic in the name,
It breathes a strange and Scandinavian sound.
No Gaelic sponsors to thy Christening came;
Dour Norsemen were they from an alien ground,
How lovely o'er thy battlemented shores
Old courtier pines, and maiden birches lean,
Royally through their midst the torrent roars,
Ne'er hath God framed a more majestic scene.

Pearls of some little value have been found in the Black Burn and human remains were taken from the Scion Tumulus near Little Mill – so called from the Gaelic 'Shian', a green fairy knoll. There are two churches, one endowed and three public schools.

Aldearn (Auld Nairn): This parish occupies the north eastern portion of the county. It has a population of 1,292 while the Parliamentary voters number 71. Its rental approaches £11,000 and it possesses two churches and three public schools. The district is principally agricultural, consisting of fine farms with here and there stretches of woodland. The village, though now of but small dimensions, was once the most important town in the county and we read of the Dean of the college in connection with Elgin Cathedral being its minister; Nairn, being attached in the form of a vicarage, was possessed simply of a chapel.

On the 9th May 1645 it was the scene of a disastrous conflict in the Covenanting Cause between Montrose and General Hurry. The centre of the Royalist army occupied the village and was supported by the two wings on either side. Its first fortune favoured the Covenanters, but chiefly owing to the spirited attack by Lord Gordon, aided by a blundered movement on their part, they were signally defeated and slain in great numbers. A few were interred in the adjoining graveyard and the remainder were buried in what is still known as the Dead Wood.

The fairest wreaths are due though never paid
To those who, posted at the Shrine of Truth,
Have fallen in her defence . . .
. . . Their blood was shed
In confirmation of the noblest claim –
To walk with God, to be divinely free,
To soar, and to anticipate the skies,
Yet few remember them. They lived unknown,
Till persecution dragged them into fame
And chased them up to Heaven.

Near this, at New Mill, is the 'Clattering Brigg' under which the Rev. Mr. Hog, Minister of Kiltearn, is said on one occasion to have taken refuge from the pursuit of the Royalist dragoons, to whose deadly imprecations he listened in safety as they passed over his hiding place undiscovered.

There are some fine mansion houses in the parish including Boath, Lochloy and Lethen. The latter in former days was burned down besides being subjected to several protracted sieges on account of the attachment of its proprietor to the Covenant. Inshoch Castle, now in ruins, was formerly the stronghold of the Hays of Lochloy. They were among the most powerful families in the north, but their last representative fell at the Battle of Auldearn.

Cawdor (Calder): This parish lies in the western section of the county. It is largely occupied by moor and moss, but the land extending along the southern bank of the Nairn is light but generally fertile. The population is 1,070 and of these 44 are Parliamentary voters. Its rental is about £4,600, the principal proprietor being the Earl of Cawdor.

Cawdor's woods are extensive and the one in the vicinity of the castle is noted for its fine trees, its unusually large junipers, its wild flowers and romantic scenery along the Hermitage Burn. This stream, which rises among the Glengoulie Hills and receives the Achindown tributary, a short way above the castle, has cleft its way through the sandstone stratum scooping out for itself a narrow tortuous channel of the most picturesque description. It derives its name from the traditional belief that a rustic cell, the habitation of some ancient recluse, was situated on the summit of a projecting cliff which arises about half way from the bed of the stream. This finely wooded and beautiful ravine cannot be better described than in the slightly altered words of Scott:-

Where twines a path, in shadow hide
Round many a rocky pyramid.
Where Nature scatters free and wild
Each plant or flower, the mountain's child
With boughs that quake at every breath
Frey birch and aspen weep beneath.
Aloft the ash and warrior oak
Cast anchor in the rifted rock;
And higher yet the pine tree swings
His shattered trunk and frequent flings
Where seem the cliffs to meet on high,
His boughs athwash the narrowed sky.
Highest of all . . .
The wanderer's eye can barely view
The summer heaven's delicious blue
So wondrous wild the whole might seem
The scenery of a fairy dream.

Near the mouth stands the old castle of Cawdor, the most perfect example of a feudal fortress in the north. Its weather-beaten tower, built over the hawthorn tree, 'its donjon keep, the loop hole grates where captives wept', encircled by more modern additions, are all enclosed within a moat, still spanned by a drawbridge which now rattles on its chains as in days of yore. Within is the room where it is said King Duncan succumbed to the dagger of Macbeth. Between the ceiling and the roof is shown 'the hole' where Lord Lovat was hid for a short time after the Battle of Culloden. The old kitchen, the tapestried walls, the carved mantlepieces and the iron-grated door from Lochindorb Castle, are all carefully preserved. In the grounds are a magnificent ash 26 feet in circumference, an unusually large yew tree and, till lately, a small flock of the old British breed of sheep.

The village of Cawdor just under the wing of the Castle is a burgh of barony, having the right to be regulated by its own officers and to hold a great annual fair in July. The parish church was the private chapel, at the door of which may still be seen the 'jouns' used for the punishment of ecclesiastical offenders.

Among other antiquarian objects of interest we may mention the vitrified fort of Auchindown, the graveyard of Barevan with its strength-testing stone – 'the clans' putting stone' – and its anciently dated monument (1 A.D.?), the supposed Druidical monolith at Balinrait, and also a few cup-marked stones over the parish. At Tomnahoolie among the prehistoric remains, were found a specimen or two of a rare chissel-shaped bone weapon, now lying in the British Museum. The famous Royal Brackla Distillery supplies whisky to many Scotchmen all over the world.

Croy: About one half of this parish only lies in the county of Nairn. The population is 1,671 and the Parliamentary voters number 36. The chief proprietor is Major Rose of Kilravock.

Along the valley of the Nairn it is generally flat and fertile but beyond is, as a rule, bare and bleak. Wide tracts of barren land are fast being reclaimed by the plough or planted with trees. Towards the western boundary lies the Loch of the Clans, the site of an ancient crannog. Delightfully situated on the western bank of the Nairn is Kilravock Castle, the fine old seat of the ancient family of Rose. Its tower is almost coeval with that of Cawdor. The barons were among the most powerful in the Highlands and the castle still contains a valuable collection of old paintings, armour and writings, among which is a papal bull for the dispensation of sins.

Two days before the Battle of Culloden Prince Charlie was here entertained by the baron at whose town house in Nairn the Duke of Cumberland had at the same time taken up his abode. Next day it was visited by the latter and immediately thereafter the baron's two guests met on the field of Culloden.

The prehistoric remains at Clava, the mysterious cup markings and the great conglomerate boulder of Tomriach are valuable examples of the ancient tumuli and the still earlier glacial action.

Nairn: This parish occupies the north western section of the county and includes the burgh. The rental of £8,000 is collected by a large number of proprietors. To the south the land is fairly rich, but towards the north it is light and sandy, and with the exception of a few acres of woodland here and there is almost completely under cultivation. The objects of greatest interest in the parish are the ruins of Castles Rait and Finlay. The former was anciently a seat of the Mackintoshes, though at an earlier period it belonged to a 'Rait of that Ilk'. Local tradition ascribes to it the scene of a great tragedy in which the Mackintoshes, by suddenly overpowering their assailants the Comyns, escaped the fate that otherwise would have befallen them. Since then the castle has remained desolate. Not far from this, forming a conical mound, is Castle Finlay, once a vitrified fort, but now almost entirely overgrown with moss. The position of this ruin supports the theory that such were used as hill fortifications.

Moy and Dalarossie: Of the parish of Moy and Dalarossie there are about 5000 acres in Nairnshire itself. It is totally a hilly and pastoral region except where transected by the river Findhorn, affording along its banks but slight opportunity for cultivation.

The Burgh of Nairn: Originally called Invernairn, it is situated on the sea coast at the mouth of the river from which it derives its name. Its resident population amounts to about 4,600 and numbers 368 Parliamentary voters. It unites with Inverness, Forres and Fortrose in returning a member of Parliament, while the county combines with Morayshire for the same purpose.

Favoured as it is by a mild climate, it also presents advantages for bathing, greatly developed within late years by possessing baths fitted up in the most approved and varied manner, and also a swimming bath, the largest and best in Scotland. The beach consists of fine sand, pleasant to tread, concealing no quicksands and gradually dipping into the sea, while the currents are so equable as to be by no means dangerous. In case of accident however, a boat provided with life-saving apparatus is at hand. Pleasant promenades have been formed on the links and, in the centre, a bandstand has recently been erected where sweet music is frequently discoursed. At such a time, while the frame may be invigorated by the cool sea breeze, the ear and the eye are both charmed: the former by the melodious sounds issuing from the orchestra, the latter by the glorious panorama stretching away to the north west.

Although Nairn continued to present an antiquated aspect to a later period than many other of our Scotch cities, it has within recent years, not only overtaken the general progress but even become an example of still greater achievement. Every vestige of age is fast disappearing. No longer are the gables of the houses suffered to deteriorate the appearance of the High Street. Almost without exception they are of the past, and in their place have been reared edifices as handsome and commodious as they are beautiful and imposing. Towards the seaside the extension of late years has been vast, and the buildings are all of the most approved and pleasing architecture.

The hotels, boarding houses and general conveniences for visitors are of a very superior description, and the Highland Railway passes on the outskirts affording easy access both to the south and north.

Water of the purest kind is supplied direct from the Geddes springs and sewage arrangements have lately been successfully carried out, thus rendering what was healthy before now doubly secure from disease and epidemics. The great problem too as to the ultimate disposal of the town sewage is being satisfactorily solved by the favourable results obtained from the management of a small farm belonging to the municipality. The town is regulated by its own magistrates – provost, baillies and councillors and the usual functionaries connected with such. A sheriff court sits once a week, but owing to the decrease of crime within the county, the prison has been removed to Inverness. A considerable estate belongs to the town, much reduced however from its original extent. Lately it has relapsed to its former possessors after the expiry of the long lease of 90 years.

Convenient as it is for approach on land, Nairn is also accessible by sea to vessels of light draught, and to afford increased facility in this respect, a new concrete pier has recently been erected on the east side of the harbour. It also gives every advantage for the successful prosecution of the white and salmon fisheries. The pursuit of these forms is the livelihood of a large portion of the total number of the inhabitants; but they live quite apart and, save in commercial matters, have but little intercourse with any outside their own pale.

With respect to churches, Nairn has no lack, having no fewer than seven, and all of different denominations. The new Free Church, built at a cost of over £7,000 is an exceedingly handsome erection, standing on and adorning the southern portion of the High Street. Of the educational institutions, the Academy comes first. It has been endowed by public subscription, aided by a donation of £2,000 from the late Captain Rose Troup. There are three board schools – the Church Street, Links and Monitory.

From among the various clubs and societies in the town there may be mentioned the Literary Institute which possesses a Library and Museum, the Nairn Artillery Volunteers, the Cricket Club, and the Games Association. In connexion with this latter are the annual Athletic Sports to which the people congregate in great numbers from the neighbouring districts and which certainly of their kind are deservedly the most popular in the North. It has also a well conducted Newspaper – the Nairnshire Telegraph – published once a week.

The Museum which stands on the High Street contains a fairly extensive and interesting collection of local antiquities, geological and botanical specimens. The minerals from Greenland are especially valuable and their history is remarkable as having been seized and brought to this country during the excitement of a European war.

The Town and County Hospital, supported by voluntary contributions, has proved of incalculable value to the poor of the district and is successfully conducted by the local medical gentlemen, who give their services without fee or reward.

Summary.

A century ago both the face of the country and the social condition of the people exhibited a marked contrast to that which obtains in the present day. Instead of the broad fields which annually yield a rich reward for the industry of the husbandman, broom, whins and heather occupied a vast extent and afforded excellent cover to vermin of all sorts. The miserable turf-built huts and the sallow complexions of the occupants told that peat reek was almost a constant element of the atmosphere within. The value of fresh air and ventilation were quite unknown. At the door of every dwelling was to be found an offensive dung heap, which along with the untidy habits common to most, was the frequent cause of trouble and disease now exceedingly rare. As drainage and the value of lime came to be understood about 50 years ago, the small crofts which afforded a scanty subsistence and a good excuse for indolence, were gradually enlarged and rendered more productive.

The harvests which formed a laborious toil for many weeks, were reaped with the sickle, and the grain was separated by the flail, dried in a home kiln and ground into an inferior meal in a rude district mill. The tenants were bound to patronise the estate miller who retained his own charge of ‘moulter’ from the amount prepared. The ‘caprin’, or poor of the parish were permitted to hang up a bag in the mill and gratefully received whatever the more charitable farmers might care to put in. The panniered Highland Shalty pony was the common beast of burden and a small but hardy breed of cattle grazed upon the moorland. The mass of the people seldom received more than the merest elements of an education, and superstition in consequence exercised a powerful influence over the popular mind. The Bible was read and sincerely respected, but the literature of the ‘chap book’, together with the ballad and legends of former days did much to cramp the general intelligence. Local fairs, in conjunction with the itinerant pack-merchant not only supplied the community with most kinds of domestic necessities but formed a very inferior medium of spreading the general news of the day from one locality to another. It is only 73 years ago since the first coach was put upon the road between Aberdeen and Inverness. The enterprise was looked upon as a doubtful one and the price of correspondence was high, but a penny post with relative fast trains and almost instantaneous telegraphic communications were results which the most speculative never dreamed of.

The state of society in the town and county of Nairn advanced with rapid strides within recent years. Since the introduction of the railway the former has developed almost at one bound into the far famed 'Brighton of the North'. Its beautiful villas, busy thoroughfares and gay promenades betoken the great social change which has been wrought in the mind and condition of its inhabitants. The improved breeds of cattle and horses combined with the rotation of cropping, the traction engine, corn reaper and other kindred agricultural inventions have raised the rural classes to a degree of refinement never before attained by them in this country.

The physical aspect of the county has also been entirely remodelled. The holdings have been enlarged and greatly improved in every respect; excellent roads permeate into the remotest corners, and the trampled sons of toil have totally disappeared. Both the farm servant and the skilled artisan have had their working hours properly regulated and their life greatly sweetened by the application of mechanical power to every department of labour. The numerous public schools, forming centres of light and culture, are providing an education for the meanest child and helping to lay the foundation of even greater benefits to the rising generation. The Celt and the Saxon are long ago blended together in peaceful harmony and their descendants of today unite the dignity of the former with the refinement of the latter in the generous nobility of character which distinguishes the native of Nairnshire both at home and abroad.

APPENDIX B

The Arctic Lecture of Robert Thomson Jnr.

Delivered to the Nairn Literary Institute on 15th October 1886 and read by his father to the Ardclach community on 26th January 1887.

When I was a student of medicine I was fortunate enough to secure a berth on board the steam whaler 'Resolute' of Dundee. My duty was to act as Surgeon during the round voyage (January to October 1895), in the course of which we were first of all to engage in the seal fishing off Newfoundland, and afterwards in the whale fishing to the west of Greenland.

The ship which was my home during that long cruise of nine months was some 500 tons register, with a displacement of about 900 tons, and was built after the usual whaler type. She was fully rigged for sailing so that coal might be economised during the long Greenland voyage, and a two-bladed screw was employed, which could be so adjusted with the blades set perpendicularly, that it interfered but little with the speed of the vessel when under canvas. The hull was strongly built with a powerful framework of heavy beams, so braced as to withstand a great pressure, while the bow was sheathed with iron plates. She was fitted with compound engines, and under steam could go a matter of eight or nine knots an hour.

Resolute

On the top of the main mast was placed the 'crow's nest', which is simply a barrel with a little trap door in the bottom by means of which access to it is obtained. It is approached from the top-yard by what is known as 'Jacob's ladder'. When working among ice, or during the whaling, a man was always stationed there whose duty it was, with the aid of a glass, to note the drifting of the ice-floes, to give the alarm if danger impended, or to rouse the crew if a whale were sighted blowing in the offing. At first the feeling is rather strange perched so high above the water, especially when the ship is rolling, for one is in constant dread of the whole business capsizing. A little experience however, soon rules off these preliminary sensations. We carried nine whale boats and a steam launch, and during the whaling a crew of sixty men all told; but at the sealing there were some three hundred men on board.

We left Dundee about the middle of January, and had a rather stormy passage across the Atlantic. Within about two hundred miles of the coast of Newfoundland we entered the vast ice fields which are annually brought south by the Arctic current. Innumerable pieces of these, while hugging the shores of Labrador, find their way through the Straits of Belle Isle into the Gulf of St Lawrence, spreading in all directions the severity of a Polar winter, and at the same time blocking the mouth of the river so completely that any commerce through the medium of shipping is entirely out of the question. The ice, which has been broken up by the swell of the ocean into pieces (or 'pans' as they are called) varying from a few square yards to over a rood or so, is usually about six to eight feet thick, covered with snow and presenting a rough uneven surface to the eye. Through these the 'Resolute' made very slow headway, incessantly wedging aside the icy masses, and frequently having to go astern so as, by moving forward again with an increasing momentum, to ram and crush them through. She was held on her zigzag course in this manner during four days, laboriously steered by relays of hardy seamen, four of whom toiled night and day almost without intermission at the wheels, in obedience to instructions from the masthead by the man in the crow's nest.

For three months we were engaged more or less in the sealing within a short distance of St John's. Here we were particularly fortunate capturing in two trips no fewer than forty thousand seals. Having discharged these we fitted out for the second part of our voyage and on the 18th of May we left for the Far North – for those regions rendered famous by the efforts of Franklin and other Arctic navigators in that vain attempt to discover a North West Passage of commercial utility which should afford an alternative route to the countries of the East.

Our course after leaving Newfoundland was in a north-easterly direction for several days, through those banks of fog so prevalent in that part. They lay so thick that it was impossible to see a half ship's length ahead. They are caused by the cold Arctic current charged with icebergs meeting the warm waters of the Gulf Stream. This portion of the passage was therefore far from agreeable. Everything was dank and musty. During the day there were no cheering rays from the sun and during the night the darkness was dismal. Meantime of course, we had to proceed with caution to avoid the possibility of collision with heavy ice. In two or three days however, we emerged into the clear atmosphere which, during the summer season, is a constant feature of northern latitudes. In fact the climate is so dry, so crisp, so exhilarating that it is quite a possibility that Greenland may yet become a sanitorium for the world, where there may be no danger of being choked with smoke, and chilled with rain, but where one may enjoy a cool, bright atmosphere in unbroken continuity.

After a sail of ten days, we hove in sight of the rocky highland on the Greenland coast. Here, on the last night, the sun just dipped into the horizon and rose to set no more with us for the long period of over three months. Probably that will constitute about the longest day of my life – a day into which were crowded so many experiences at once unique and interesting.

The sea was calm as a millpond, while over its surface, protruding their rugged outlines, were scattered icebergs as far as the eye could reach. Away to the right was the Greenland shore crowned with glaciers, slowly but surely grinding their way to the sea. And now the sun sank into a hazy bed of vapour on the northern horizon. The whole seascape was suffused with a red glow, flooding the ocean with its fiery light, tinting the icebergs as with gold, and reflecting its warm colours in strange contrast against the cold, snowy sea-board in the distance. It formed a spectacle of magic beauty well fitted to impress the mind as one of many pleasing recollections of the wonderful phenomena to be witnessed in these frozen regions.

We came across some walruses basking in the sun on stray pieces of ice and, having shot a few, we made a start with our oil cargo from the fat obtained on their carcasses. The hide is of considerable value as it is thick and very tough, while the tusks are of use for the purpose of fashioning small objects in ivory. They are rather dangerous brutes to tackle especially when wounded, for when roused they do not hesitate to attack a boat, which they would speedily wreck with their powerful tusks. Their skulls are so thick and hard that ordinary bullets seldom penetrate, but are merely flattened against them doing little harm.

At last we sighted the island of Disco, rising like a huge round mountain right ahead, and in a few hours more the 'Resolute' was safely moored by means of her ice anchors in the little land-locked bay, which forms the harbour for the small Danish settlement of Lievely. The rocks around are about destitute of vegetation, but bear very distict tracings of glacial action. The settlement consists of a score or two of turf huts, scarcely to be recognised at a short distance from the soil on which they stand, along with two or three wooden erections forming the residences of the Governor and Inspector. We had a visit from these officials, who are always ready to welcome a passing whaler, relieving as it does for a little, the dull monotony of their existence, exiled from home and from friends. The inhabitants are mostly half-breeds and eke out a precarious subsistence by bartering the spoils of the chase (in the form of skins, fat and ivory) with the Danish authorities in return for biscuit, coffee, tobacco and a few other luxuries of civilised life. The government maintains a blacksmith, a carpenter and cooper to assist the natives; and also a schoolmaster to teach the children to read and write the Danish language.

We saw great numbers of dogs used for the purpose of pulling their sleighs in winter, but at that time they were off duty, and kept up a continual fighting and howling. In size they resemble the Scotch collie, but their sharply-pointed ears give them very much a wolfish appearance. We noted here in a very marked degree, the defect common to the whole canine race in these northern parts as well as on the opposite shores of Labrador; they yelp and howl in the most dismal manner, but are totally silent as to the power of barking. This accomplishment, so common among the domestic dogs of our country, they very readily acquire if brought for any length of time into contact with these.

Here we met the man who acted as dog driver in the 'Alert' and 'Discovery' Polar expedition under Sir George Nares. He took great pride in exhibiting the testimonials he received from his superiors on their return from that perilous enterprise among the everlasting ice. It may be mentioned that this same man, on another occasion, was among a party of fourteen who, getting separated from the American ship 'Polaris' in the Davis Straits, drifted south on the pack ice and survived all the hardships of their terrible position till they were rescued near the Straits of Belle Isle, off the coast of Newfoundland.

After spending some twelve hours we took our departure and, in company with the 'Arctic', coasted northwards keeping as close to the shore as possible. Nowhere is there a break in the precipitous character of the rocks which rise one to two thousand feet sheer from the sea. Every valley is filled with its glacier, slowly driven downward by the enormous pressure from behind. These often extend far into the water and constitute the never-failing source of numerous icebergs, which crowd the seas and endanger navigation even far south into the Atlantic. Inland we know, from Dr Nansen, that this great continent is one dreary expanse of ice; a mighty glacier formed by the accumulated snow of ages which, rising to a height of some nine thousand feet, overtops the highest mountains, burying them out of sight.

About two hundred miles north from Disco, we called at the Danish settlement of Upernavik – the most northerly civilised station in the world, as I was led to understand. In appearance it is much the same as the one we had just left. It occupies one or two of a small group of islands, and is possessed of a fairly good harbour. The snow had just melted leaving it bare and desolate, and impressed me strongly with the idea that it had just arisen out of the sea. Here, as elsewhere, the natives came aboard to barter slippers and tobacco pouches, made from sealskin, in return for tobacco or any article of small value with which one was disposed to trade. During our short stay, a native came in, reporting ten whalers lying thirteen miles further north, barred from all progress by the ice.

After leaving Upernavik, we entered upon the most dangerous part of the voyage. Great care had to be exercised in directing the vessel's course, so as to avoid being nipped among the numerous floes which were drifting southwards. We zigzagged and doubled in the most erratic manner, but nevertheless steadily gained ground and came up at length to what appeared unbroken ice. Berthed along its edge we found the rest of the whaling fleet lying like vessels at a quay. We were in the vicinity of the group known as the Duck Islands, where the eider duck congregate in large numbers and where, in the season, great quantities of valuable down (with which the birds form their nests) may be obtained.

Notwithstanding our great precautions, we had one evening a taste of being nipped in the sea. Both the 'Arctic' and the 'Resolute' were lying not far apart and apparently quite safe in an open space of water between two very extensive floes. As there was no visible agency on the surface everyone forgot that there might be a far more powerful influence at work in the under currents. In our position it would have taken one or two hours under full steam to escape from between the expanded jaws of solid ice. Our dismay may therefore be imagined when it became unmistakably evident that the edges were slowly closing up under a momentum so practically irresistible that both ships were face to face with impending destruction. The loss of all our belongings was comparatively but a slight matter; our lives alone might be saved should we all succeed in scrambling over the ice to the shelter of one or other of the whalers which might be within reach. In spite of an effort to slip from between the closing masses, the stern of the 'Resolute' was at length grasped as in the throat of a mighty shears. For ten minutes the squeezing, grinding process went on, and it seemed as if our ship must be entombed in the mountain ridge of slush, ice and snow, which was piling up like a wall and marked the junction of the two opposing fields, far far astern. Gradually however, and as the last rays of hope were dying away, the pressure eased off and fortunately ceased altogether. In a few minutes all hands were at work digging and blasting her out, and in a short time she was set free. As she nobly steamed away, little the worse of the terrible danger which had threatened her, we were all again enabled to breathe more freely.

After many delays and much manoeuvring we reached the south and of Melville Bay, that bay which is commonly the dread of Arctic navigators but which at times, like the Bay of Biscay, belies its reputation. To our disappointment, a great sheet of ice six to eight feet thick – which is the usual thickness of ice one winter old – lay right across our bow. This completely blocked our entrance into a narrow lead a quarter of a mile away, which could be seen communicating with a great expanse of clear water beyond. It was decided to force the barrier by means of ramming. Steaming up against the floe at full speed, taking turn about with the 'Arctic' and the 'Esquimaux' (each in succession crushing through half a ship's length), in three hours the 'Resolute' and her two consorts entered an interminable space of open sea. We had an uniterrupted run through Melville Bay, which proved most enjoyable, and we sighted the Devil's Thumb, a very lofty rock on the coast, standing out in solitary grandeur. Soon after, Dalrymple Rock on the north west extremity of the Bay appeared. It is a small but precipitous island lying close under the mainland, and forms a favourite resort for all kinds of Arctic fowl hatching their young. Hundreds of dozens of eggs may be gathered here, a boat's crew being commonly sent ashore for the purpose. But we did not put off steam so Cape York and the mainland were soon left far astern.

While in the latitude of Carey Islands, my attention was directed to one of the mightiest glaciers in the world, stretching out five or six miles in breadth. From time to time, masses of colossal dimensions break off, and there is an almost continuous cannonade of smaller fragments. It looks like a mountain barrier of enormous extent, rising inland to a great height and, notwithstanding its heavy losses at the marine end, is so regularly augmented from behind that no change is perceptible from age to age. It was with mixed feeling engendered of awe and wonder that I gazed on this monument of Arctic grandeur, and felt assured that no such panorama would again confront my astonished senses.

The Carey Islands – which was the highest latitude reached by any of the whalers in 1885 – were touched on the 13th of June. They consist of a number of bare rocks of considerable size, and frequented by seafowl in large numbers for the purpose of hatching their young. The largest of the group was considered by the relief expedition, a very likely point of convenience for depositing some time previously a few useful stores on behalf of Lieutenant Greely, then in command of the American Polar Expedition. There was reason to believe however, from the statement of one of our seamen who had been there the year before, that the rum cask, if tapped, would show rather a diminished ankerage since it left the States' vessel. Indeed now that the gallant Lieutenant had got back all safe and sound, there was some talk on board the 'Resolute' of putting the matter beyond all doubt. But in the end wiser and better counsels prevailed and, so far as we were concerned, the stores were left untouched, perchance to prove a welcome find to some starving explorer.

From Carey Islands the ship's course was directed towards Lancaster Sound, on the south west. For several weeks we had been striving to overcome one difficulty after another, but the worst was now past and we were soon steaming up the Sound in open water towards Barrow Straits. Having sailed as far as Leopold Island on the north western extremity of Prince Regent's Inlet, the floe again barred our further progress. We had however, reached far enough, and the ship was consequently berthed against the ice. Every preparation was then made for commencing the whale fishery in earnest. A couple of boats were always kept at watch . . . At the same time the man in the crow's nest kept a sharp lookout in all directions for the peculiar blast of vapour indicative of a huge whale making its way to the ice. For about three weeks our utmost endeavours were spent in vain, notwithstanding many hopes and weary chases in pursuit of one or more which occasionally rose almost within our reach.

Early one morning however, a whale was signalled from the masthead. Immediately orders were given to have all the boats launched. A cheerful obedience was readily accorded, the men straightway tumbling out of their bunks, and rushing on deck in their sleeping suits into an atmosphere rather below freezing point, carrying their clothes to dress, as opportunity afforded, in the boats. On all such occasions there is great tumult and excitement on board as if the ship were in immediate peril. In less than three minutes the boats were manned, launched, and spread about in various directions. As good luck would have it, I myself accompanied the boats as one of the crew. Scarcely had we taken up position when a shot fired close to the ship, immediately followed by the hoisting of a flag on board; and the calling of 'A fall! A fall!' betokened to us that the whale had been fastened. In a trice we were all pulling towards the scene of action, and thereafter arranging ourselves to await the reappearance of the whale, which of course had dived immediately on being struck. There was not long to wait and, several boats being handy, another three harpoons with lines attached were speedily planted in the monster's back. Being thus securely fastened, the work which now lay before us was to despatch him with lances. Again and again he plunged beneath the surface but, on each successive reappearance, we pulled in (carefully avoiding the sweep of his huge tail with which he lashed the sea into foam) and our harpooners pierced his body with their lances. At the same time explosive rockets were fired which burst and did dreadful damage. From every wound the blood flowed in small streams, and the water all round was tinged with a purple hue. Instead of the usual breathings of vapour, columns of blood began to spout from the blowholes, and were forced at times several feet into the air, drenching the men who chanced to be within range. It was two hours from the planting of the first blow before we withdrew beyond the reach of the last struggle – when the dying monster in his death agony rolled and plunged to free himself from the cruel harpoons and the lines with which he was now hopelessly entangled. Then his mighty frame quivered in a few convulsive throes and, quite exhausted, he turned over on his back and expired.

It was then found to be a full-sized specimen of the Black Whale, as it is usually called, found only in the seas of the Far North, and frequently called the Right Whale, to distinguish it from the Fin-backed variety, which also haunts the nothern waters. The Finner, though often attaining greater size than the Black Whale, is only of slight commercial value, being extremely dangerous to meddle with, while the carcass yields but little fat or whalebone. The length of our whale was about 60 feet, with a weight of about 150 tons. The body was made fast to the ship's side by means of chains, and the process of flensing was at once commenced. A few of the men, having their boots armed with iron spikes to prevent their slipping, got down upon the back and cut into the blubber removing, one after another, broad strips or blankets twenty to thirty feet long until the fat was entirely removed. Meantime the mouth was stripped of its whalebone, or baleen as it is more properly called. It is by means of this that the whale procures its sustenance. Filling its huge mouth with water, which teems with minute gelatinous organisms, it then squirts it out through the long hair which fringes the plates of whalebone. In the hairy meshes these organisms are caught and, being now swallowed, constitute the food of the whole. So strange is it that, in the natural economy, this huge monster should be dependent for its nourishment on such minute forms of life. Altogether this whale yielded about 18 tons of oil, and some 17 hundredweights of whalebone. This represented a total value of about £2500, for at the present day whalebone is a most valuable commodity, and commands from two to three thousand pounds a ton. The remainder of the carcass was then cast adrift on the wide sea, and became doubtless a welcome source of revel and high carnival to the sharks beneath as well as to the birds and even bears above the surface of the water.

During the operation of flensing, the large pieces of fat are simply lowered to the 'tween decks as they are removed from the body, but subsequently, when all is over and the men have had a few hours rest, all hands are summoned again for the purpose of 'making off' as the whalers have it. This consists of hoisting each of the pieces on deck where the rind or skin is pared off with a sharp blubber spade and the fat cut into cubes of about a foot. These are again placed upon a board, chopped very small, and passed through a canvas tube into the tanks below which, when filled, are screwed up and the contents untouched until removed to the oil factories in Dundee.

The remuneration of the crew, in addition to a small wage, depends upon a ship's catch during the season. In addition to this – the more to stimulate their interest – a premium is awarded to the harpooner and his crew who first succeed in fastening a whale. Among our harpooners was an old man of very great experience who had seen Sir John Franklin in the Straits in 1845 when, with the 'Erebus' and 'Terror', he went in search of the North West Passage. Since that time he had harpooned no fewer than a hundred whales, whose aggregate value he estimated to be a hundred thousand pounds.

Soon after our last capture, a more than usually disappointing chase followed. One of our boats, while away about a mile from the ship, succeeded in fixing their harpoon in a huge female whale which was accompanied by her young sucker. No sooner had the crew hoisted their small signal flag in token of their success and need of help, than the 'Resolute' responded by immediately despatching a couple of boats to stand by and render whatever assistance might be found necessary. Three or four more pulled off to arrange themselves over as wide a space as possible, awaiting her reappearance. As in all such cases of family companionship, the men were warned to refrain from meddling on any condition with the young one until the mother had been effectually secured. The reason as they all knew, was the great risk which is thereby incurred of arousing in the parent her maternal anxieties. The appearance therefore of a signal displayed from another boat, led us to imagine that they had been fortunate enough to get a second harpoon planted in the whale, and thus we caused all the free boats to pull away to its assistance. To our great disappointment the old salts soon discovered that the young one had been fastened instead of the mother. On being hauled in it was found to be quite dead, and when hoisted aboard it yielded us some two tons of very fine oil. As this was the harpooner's first visit to the Polar seas it ought in justice to be stated on his behalf that it requires an experienced eye to be able to distinguish the one from the other on account of the small portion of the back which is exposed above the surface in the act of breathing. During this unlucky diversion the parent came up in an unguarded spot, regaled her lungs with air, and then betook herself again to the depths. With dejected hearts as well as exhausted energies the crews were at length compelled to desist, and the 'Resolute' was reluctantly headed round for the floe edge in the hope of better fortune in the future. The loss must have been well over £2000. But by this time it was found that more than two miles of line had been run out, and that either the harpoon must have drawn, or the rope broken – a circumstance which would have seriously crippled the vessel by the loss of such a length of cordage. On our return there was no help for it but to set about hauling in the empty line. Accordingly the men got out upon the ice, and began the dreary work. I can imagine nothing more intensely disagreeable than the continued weary toil of passing a wet, icy rope through the hands, and again recoiling it in the boats. After four hours of this drudgery, it was at least satisfactory to find that every inch was recovered, even the harpoon itself, shapelessly twisted.

We met with the Arctic Gulls in countless numbers, and specially amongst them the Fulmar Petrels, or 'Malleys' as they are commonly called. This one which is so well known to Polar voyagers is a rather handsome creature, and has many queer ways of its own. Whenever they heard the crack of our rifles and saw the snow stained with blood, they were sure to present themselves in daring multitudes. They appear to possess acutely the sense of both sight and smell, for on several occasions when lying becalmed with not a single bird within range of our vision, no sooner had we secured a haul of fat than in a few minutes they were winging around with delighted screams. A morsel of flesh thrown overboard has so great attractions that a couple of dozen might be seen striving for it within a square yard. After having secured enough, they may be seen rising up into the air sailing round and around, enjoying themselves, and shrieking out their satisfaction. Now is the time for another marauder to appear on the scene. This is the Skua Gull, a bold, black, hawklike rascal which seldom comes within gunshot of our ship. He is wild as the North Wind itself, and forthwith he singles out and swoops down upon one of the revellers. He is innocent of murderous intent, but keeps up a relentless pursuit until at length his victim, sorely distressed, disgorges some of its late plunder, which straightway he catches up like a flash ere it reaches the water. On this the Skua lives because his organs can only assimilate food which has been already partially digested by others. No wonder therfore that the Greenlanders call him an unclean bird.

The 'Malleys' however, wild and voracious though they be, are invested with a halo of superstitious regard, which is only now beginning to die away. The great majority of our seamen looked upon a wanton injury done to any fulmar as an ill omen . . . Even on board the 'Resolute' there were from time to time a few croakings should any of us venture to let fly at a passing Malley. When out on the ice myself and in the absence of more legitimate game an unfortunate stray one chanced to fall to my gun, out of consideration for my companions' feelings, I invariably consigned its sacred carcass to a hidden recess beyond the possibility of discovery. The origin however, of this regard is easily understood. Many times they have been instrumental in directing observation to a dead whale for, owing to the thousands which gather over the carrion and the wild shrieks they emit in their fierce quarrels, they can scarcely fail to attract the attention of any passing vessel.

In the course of our movements through Lancaster Sound, we visited the Loomery of Cape Hay. It is probably one of the largest auk colonies in the world, and is situated on a huge cliff which rises sheer up from the sea to a height of about nine hundred feet. On the lower ledges the Looms [Guillemots] form their nests and hatch their young. The numbers which make this their chief place of resort are almost inconceivable. If suddenly startled, close under the rock, by gunshot for instance, they rise and wheel about overhead in such overwhelming multitude that the sky is overcast as with a thick cloud, and the light of day is perceptibly diminished. They are most expert divers, and if pursued on the water, instead of taking to flight as might be expected, will persistently dive under the surface in the most remarkable manner. To many of the seamen their flesh formed a palatable dish, though rather strong and fishy-flavoured. Still it must no doubt prove a welcome change to those who are accustomed mostly to salt provisions for weeks on end.

During most of the trip I had frequently heard of and longed for a sight of the great Polar Bear and listened to many blood-curdling tales of their prowess and of the danger of being attacked by them on the ice. Occasionally on our way north we caught a glimpse of one or more, but always at such a distance as rendered it extremely unsafe to hunt them on those ever-changing, ever drifting floes. I must confess I always took the precaution of carrying a rifle when making a lengthy excursion on the ice. I have the notion that a bear has even a stronger dislike to a personal interview than I had myself. Only once at least did we get within range. We were tacking about in Pond's Bay under easy canvas when a bear was espied not far away swimming in the open water. At the time we must have been fully 30 miles from the nearest land and, no ice being within short reach, Bruin had nowhere left to betake himself for refuge. A boat was lowered and we set off in pursuit. Expert swimmers though they are, this one was no match for the crew of a whaleboat and finding himself overhauled, he faced round. Growling savagely he bit and tore in his baffled rage at the oars and the gunwhale of the boat. A bullet in the neck quickly despatched him and we towed him to the ship to hoist him aboard. Out of the water he appeared a big powerful animal with white hairy coat and strong claws and teeth, altogether such an appearance as was calculated to impress one with a wholesome respect for his kind.

As the midnight sun was now dipping nearer and nearer to the northern horizon, we were daily reminded that the season was fast drawing to a close. There was still room in the tanks for more oil, and as our fortunes in respect of the Right Whale had seemingly come to an end, we turned our attention to the capture of the White Whale – an occasional visitor to our British seas. It is a very small Cetacean belonging to the Dolphin family, and attains a length of only some 12 to 15 feet. It lives chiefly on fish, but is very fond of salmon, which they may be seen pursuing in large numbers up the mouths of tidal rivers. Elwin Bay in Prince Regent's Inlet has a splendid shallow estuary, suitable for grounding them at low water, and is sometimes on that account called White Whale Bay. Here the 'Resolute' cast anchor in the offing, and waited till a school was reported to have gone sufficiently far up. Whereupon we pulled off and arranged the boats so as to intercept them on the return of the tide. Gradually and with extreme watchfulness, the crews rowed after them, all the while shouting and splashing with the oars so as to terrify them if possible into the shallowest parts. Soon, as the tide commenced to ebb, they all instinctively turned their heads towards the open sea. Then began the battle, fierce and determined, as rush after rush was repulsed by means of the most terrific yelling, splashing and firing of blank shot. In a short time the herd became greatly excited, darting hither and thither in search of an outlet, lashing each other in their fear and stirring up the distracted water all around, till it boiled and foamed like a seething pot. This was a hard game to play seeing that it had to be kept up for several hours; but as the returning tide gradually decreased the general depth, they became less and less able and too exhausted to continue the struggle. The men then entered the water in their sea boots and proceeded to despatch them amid a spasmodic flopping of fins and jerking of tails. All were then tied in heaps and the ends of the ropes secured ashore. With the next tidal flow they could then be pulled up the beach and flensed at leisure. Our drive consisted of one hundred and eighty, about equal in oil to one good whale and therefore worth some £800.

In cruising about among the Polar islands on the northern extremity of America, we frequently came in contact with the native Esquimaux, who alone reside in that sterile and inhospitable region. Eskimo is a nickname received from their ancient foes the Indians, and signifies a raw flesh eater; but they are known among themselves as Invit or 'the People', their idea being that the Great Spirit made first of all the rest of the world experimentally, and then as his work of perfection created 'Invit'. Living in small nomadic groups of from 20 to 30, they are found at wide intervals along the coastline. The total number which inhabit these parts has been estimated at between three and four thousand, but a correct census is of course impossible. Whether in respect of race they ought to be classed with the Mongolians or Red Indians is still a matter of discussion among ethnologists, their language tending to place them among the latter, whereas their physiognomy presents some of the most marked characteristics of the former. The complexion in no way helps towards a solution of the problem for, when the long-standing encrustations of oil and dirt have been removed by a liberal treatment with soap and water, the skin appears decidedly white.

In height they do not average over five feet, but are stout and plump in proportion. Occasionally I have met a stalwart native who considerably exceeded these stunted dimensions. Their dress in general consists of roughly-prepared skins. In the milder season articles of more civilized clothing may at times be substituted indicating either a commercial intercourse with some of the ships or, in recent years at least, an illicit freedom with one or more of the Government stores left many years ago for Franklin. Their improvident habits render such booty of little real value to them since it is bartered at the earliest opportunity. In connection with the dress of the women, a large hood made of sealskin is worn and slung across the shoulders after the manner of a fishwife's creel. Here she invariably carries and almost entirely rears her infant. This nursing bag she utilizes as a very handy receptacle for all sorts of things such as coffee, tobacco, or bread which she may collect during her visit on board. Everything, in short, is stuffed in beside the baby, irrespective of classification or the least concern as to the previous or present contents of the pouch.

In their respective families they appear to live in terms of the greatest friendship. On every occasion the parents manifested the greatest forbearance and love towards their offspring. Corporal punishment seemed to be with them a forgotten art, and the more helpless were especially cared for by the mother.

In the summer season they live in small tents constructed of skins thrown over a rude, conical framework of short poles. But during the winter they huddle together in 'tubeks' or snow huts, which strange as it may seem, are most effectively capable of resisting the extreme cold. The interior at best must be dull or dreary, but became intolerably so to us from the stench, and vitiated atmosphere caused by the burning of a moss, saturated in oil, which is used in cooking and lighting. When dependent upon their own resources, their diet is entirely an animal one, but presents a considerable variety including seal, salmon, bear, loom and reindeer. These last they hunt in the autumn and store up the flesh as their mainstay against the coming winter, while the skins are converted to garments. They eat their food raw or only partially cooked, while to all but particularly to the parched and wearied huntsman, a draught of blood freshly drawn from the veins of his victim, is a luxury so prized and delicious as in itself almost to repay him for the toils of the chase. Shut off as they are from the civilized world within a limitless expanse of snowclad wastes, they eagerly look forward to the arrival of the whale ships as affording them a market for their bear skins and ivory. By previous contract invariably entered into at the commencement of each voyage, such barter is entirely restricted to the master, who trades solely in the interests of the owners.

Their usual mode of locomotion is by means of sleighs each drawn by teams of from six to ten dogs. During the long winter night in the fitful light of the Aurora Borealis, they make excursions round and about the numerous inlets and bays which intersect and break up the northern coast. The whip they use is itself unique. To the short handle about 14 inches in length is attached a long and heavy lash some 15 feet or more, with which the driver from his seat can touch up each laggard dog with unerring precision.

In the summer season the whole time of the man is devoted either to hunting or fishing. For the latter occupation each man is provided with a tiny kaiak. It is constructed of a light framework of wood, over which sealskin is stretched and sewn together with the sinew of the reindeer. This forms a covering, tense and absolutely impervious to the water. They are usually about 17 feet long, tapering gracefully away at both ends, with an opening in the centre just large enough to fit the man's thighs. The points are armed with knobs of bone, and strips of bone run along the exterior to protect it from being torn by the ice or from injury when drawn up the beach. The whole is so light that with its fittings, it may be easily carried over the floe, or across an isthmus of land. Seated above in this frail craft, the kaiaksman commits himself to the mercy of the waves, and boldly attacks with success the smaller mammalia of the deep such as narwhals, seals or walruses. It is said, when out in heavy weather, these expert seamen can capsize and right themselves without letting in a drop of water, the breaker meantime rolling harmlessly over them . . .

Though their lot has not been cast among the pleasant places of this earth, and though in the exigencies of their mode of life, they are often reduced to a hand to mouth existence, yet they always appear in the best of humour, smiling and happy, and disturbed with no thoughts about the cares of the morrow. In their primitive existence indeed, if they lack the nobler aspirations, if they lack the higher feelings engendered in civilized life, they are at least free from its endless worries, its high pressure and its constant strife.

Meantime we proceeded slowly southwards, and beyond the Arctic Circle. The lengthening nights, now accompanied by intermittent frosts, gave unmistakable evidence that the whole northern zone was soon again to be bound up in the icy embrace of a Polar winter. In these circumstances our departure was decided on and, on the 22nd of October amid an outburst of cheering and display of bunting, we finally weighed anchor for home. Four days later we weathered the rugged, iron-bound promontory of Cape Farewell, where we took one long and last adieu of those eternal glaciers which sleep upon its towering inland mountains. Six days thereafter on a misty morning we passed the Butt of Lewis, finally arriving in Dundee on the 12th day after our departure from Greenland.

Index